HOW TO PRAY

HOW TO STUDY THE BIBLE

HOW TO PRAY
HOW TO STUDY THE BIBLE

R.A. TORREY

HENDRICKSON
Christian
🌿 *Classics*

HENDRICKSON
PUBLISHERS

Hendrickson Publishers, Inc.
P.O. Box 3473
Peabody, Massachusetts 01961-3473

ISBN-13: 978-1-56563-817-4
ISBN-10: 1-56563-817-4

Printed in the United States

Second Printing—August 2006

CONTENTS

Contents

Preface

Hendrickson Christian Classics Edition

R.A. Torrey
(1856–1928)

Some lives are remembered as the suns on which the constellations of history spin; others are remembered as the stars that stream in their wake. Why some people fire our imaginations and become symbols of entire eras or movements, and others live on only as one of history's footnotes, is a mystery. In the nineteenth century, Dwight L. Moody was one of those larger-than-life figures, a man whose name was synonymous with evangelism and education, whose name evokes the entire era of nineteenth-century revival and birth of the movement to train Christian laypeople for service. In his wake, just as energetic and effective a servant as Moody, was R.A. Torrey, sometimes called the Elisha to Moody's Elijah.

Torrey came along side Moody to fulfill his vision for a training school, and in the process became a renowned Christian educator. He toured the world as an evangelist, served as a pastor, and authored over forty books— teachings on prayer, the Bible, the Holy Spirit, and evangelization—that are still favorites today. Torrey has been described as "a man of prayer, a student of the Bible, and an outstanding personal soul-winner." It was said that daily he read the Bible in four languages, that he had a familiar working knowledge of Greek and Hebrew. His entire life is a vivid example of a life lived in utter commitment to Jesus Christ, a fulfillment of Moody's proclamation: "The world has yet to see what God can do with a man fully consecrated to him. By God's help, I aim to be that man."

Reuben Archer Torrey was born January 28, 1856 in Hoboken, New Jersey, one of four children. His parents were Christians, his father a corporate lawyer. They led a comfortable life, first in New Jersey, then Brooklyn, then upstate New York. While Christian principles were part of his home life, young Reuben found worldly pleasures attractive, and, after he entered Yale University at the age of fifteen, dancing, cards, theater, and race tracks were regular entertainments.

Like other young college students, Torrey experienced skepticism about his faith and religious upbringing. His resistance to Christian commitment lay in large part with his almost prophetic understanding that turning to God meant that preaching, not lawyering, would become his calling. He struggled against God, even fell into a depression, until finally one night he woke up and said, "Oh, God, deliver me from this burden— I'll even preach!" He was eighteen at the time, and shortly thereafter he made a profession of faith in the Yale chapel. Later that same year (1875), he graduated and entered Yale Divinity School. He earned his B.D. in 1878 and his D.D. in 1879.

It was while at Yale Divinity School that Torrey first met the man who would so influence his life and career. It wasn't a professor or visiting scholar. Rather, it was an odd, uneducated evangelist by the name of Dwight L. Moody, right there in New Haven, Connecticut. After hearing Moody speak one night, the students—including Torrey—asked Moody, "Tell us how to win people to Jesus Christ." Moody's reply: "Go at it! That's the best way to learn." And that's what Torrey did. Telling others about Jesus Christ became his lifelong passion. Later in his life he often said, "I love to preach the Gospel of Jesus Christ." He was a long way from the young man who had so adamantly resisted God's call!

On December 5, 1878, Torrey was ordained in the Congregational Church, and became pastor of a church in Garrettsville, Ohio, a small town in northeast Ohio. Torrey married a young woman named Clara Smith in 1879, and began his family—there were five Torrey offspring—and his career in ministry. He seems to have had a talent for administration, and during his time in Ohio, Torrey applied his gifts not only to his church, but also to various organizations, like the Sunday School Union, the Temperance Society, the Republican Party, and the City Missionary Society.

Between 1882 and 1883 Torrey took a break to continue his education in Germany, at the Leipzig and Erlangen Universities. He was apparently dissatisfied with his seminary learning and wanted to focus on his biblical studies. A brilliant student, Torrey excelled in higher criticism, the then-fashionable approach to interpreting Scripture, free from church doctrine or tradition. The more he learned, however, the more unhappy Torrey became, until ultimately he returned to his orthodox views. This education refined Torrey's knowledge and thinking on the Bible, contributing to his great power as a Bible teacher and educator. Torrey would never be at the mercy of others when it came to biblical knowledge and interpretation.

When Torrey returned from Europe, he moved his family to Minneapolis, accepting the call from a poor, very small church. They began as a congregation of about a dozen members, known as the Open Door Church. He later moved to the People's Church, also in Minneapolis. In addition to his pastoral duties, Torrey also accepted the position as the superintendent of the Congregational City Mission Society. During this period of hard work and limited resources, Torrey learned powerful spiritual lessons on the power of prayer and on trusting God. It was during this time that he began the habit of holding special prayer meetings asking God for world-wide revival, and for the release of the power of his Holy Spirit.

By 1889, Torrey's work brought him to the attention of a man who was seeking someone to head his new school in Chicago. Dwight L. Moody's vision for a school to train Christian laypeople in the Bible and Christian ministry was very nearly complete. All that was needed was a strong leader, and that leader was R. A. Torrey. At age 33, Torrey became the first superintendent of the Chicago Evangelization Society, which would later become the Moody Bible Institute. He guided the school for nearly 20 years, from its opening until 1908, developing its distinctive curriculum, including the special practical Christian work component. During this period, Torrey also became the pastor of the Chicago Avenue Church (now Moody Memorial Church) where he served from 1894 to 1906. Torrey's vision, education, gifts, and experience made him the perfect man for these tasks, and ultimately raised his profile in the Christian world.

A passion for evangelism was only one thing that Torrey and Moody shared. They worked on a great variety of projects together: the school in Chicago, evangelistic campaigns, Bible conferences, and Moody's boarding schools in Northfield, Massachusetts. These two men were very different; as one person explained, "Moody was brusque, impulsive, and uneducated; Torrey polished, logical, and scholarly." As different as the two men were, they developed a lasting friendship. Torrey even built a summer home in Northfield, where the two men could be seen together early mornings driving through the countryside in a carriage. Torrey and Moody worked closely, so closely that it was Torrey who stepped in to carry on Moody's Kansas City evangelistic campaign in November 1899, when Moody collapsed a short time before his death.

Torrey's students and colleagues alike remember him as a brilliant Bible teacher, thanks to his training and continued study; and a powerful man of prayer. In keeping with his early practice, he organized prayer teams wherever he went. As part of his pastoral duties, he organized teams all over Chicago to pray for their pastor. At the Institute, there was formed a weekly prayer meeting (some three hundred strong) focused on praying for world-wide revival. Torrey and a few associates would meet after to continue praying, and after three years, Torrey received a burden to pray that God would send him around the world to preach God's salvation. Within two weeks, Torrey was approached by two strangers from Australia who asked him to come and preach "down under." The faithful prayers of many people were bearing fruit.

Torrey was granted a leave of absence from the Institute and the church, and put together an evangelistic team. In 1902, the team headed for Australia, with detours to preach in Japan and China, then finally a six-month Australian campaign with a trip to New Zealand. He accepted an invitation to Britain, and on the way, spent six weeks preaching in India. He led evangelistic meetings in England, Ireland, Wales, Scotland, France, and Germany through 1905, then, in 1906, began traveling throughout the United States and Canada, preaching and evangelizing. He concluded his touring in 1911, with a return visit to England, Scotland, and Ireland. It is estimated that by the time he ended his traveling, the teams had witnessed more than 100,000 people come to faith in Jesus Christ.

In addition to his evangelism, he found time for other godly endeavors. He founded the Montrose Bible Conference in Montrose, Pennsylvania (where later he was buried) and served as president of the United States Home Council of Africa Inland Mission. But then came the call from California, from a group of visionaries who had determined to offer laypeople on the west coast the same educational opportunities available back east. Torrey moved west to serve as dean of the Bible Institute of Los Angeles—BIOLA—in 1912, a post he held for twelve years. He'd come full circle, back to building a fine educational system. And of course, he had to preach, becoming the first pastor of the renowned Church of the Open Door (1915–1924). God continued to bless Torrey's work, as thousands were trained at BIOLA and pastored at Church of the Open Door. On top of these duties he made two evangelistic trips, one to Japan and China (1919), one to China and Korea (1921). In 1924, he retired to a life of Bible conferences and special lectures, including a stint as special lecturer at Moody Bible Institute, until his death in 1928.

Torrey's legacy includes playing a key role in the development of American Fundamentalism, and a literary treasure of over forty books. These book explore and celebrate the passions of his life: the Holy Spirit, personal evangelism, revival, prayer, and Bible study, all of which reveal the vitality and power of Torrey's life in Christ. The two titles included in this volume—How to Pray and How to Study the Bible—represent the core of Torrey's beliefs, of his entire life of obedience and service.

In the 1895 edition of the Yale class notes, called The Twenty Year Record, alumni were asked a series of questions about their lives. In response to a question about his hobbies, Torrey wrote:

> I have but one hobby: to get men to know and believe and love the Lord
> Jesus Christ, to whom I owe all the wondrous joy I know and anything

there is good in me; and to believe the Bible—the book I once doubted utterly, but now know to be the Word of God, and to give up trying to be or do anything in their own strength, and to let the Holy Spirit come in with all his fullness to do it all.

This same passion and excitement, this utter commitment to Jesus Christ, is evident in all Torrey's writing. Listen closely as you read and you will hear the vibrant voice of this extraordinary servant—and learn from him how this all can be yours as well.

How to Pray

First Published 1900

CHAPTER 1

The Importance of Prayer

In the sixth chapter of Ephesians, in the 18th verse, we read words which put the tremendous importance of prayer with startling and overwhelming force:

Praying always with all prayer and supplication in the Spirit, and watching thereunto with all perseverance and supplication for all saints.

When we stop to weigh the meaning of these words, then note the connection in which they are found, the intelligent child of God is driven to say,

I must pray, pray, pray. I must put all my energy and all my heart into prayer. Whatever else I do, I must pray.

The Revised Version [the 1885 revision of the King James Version] is, if possible, stronger than the Authorized:

With all prayer and supplication praying at all seasons in the spirit, and watching thereunto in all perseverance and supplication for all the saints.

Note the *alls*: "with *all* prayer," "at *all* seasons," "in *all* persever-ance," "for *all* the saints." Note the piling up of strong words: "prayer," "supplication," "perseverance." Note once more the strong expression, "watching thereunto"; more literally, "being sleepless thereunto." Paul realized the natural slothfulness of man, and especially his natural slothfulness in prayer. How seldom we pray things through! How often the church and the individual get right up to the verge of a great bless-ing in prayer, and just then let go, get drowsy, quit. I wish that these words "being sleepless unto prayer" might burn into our hearts. I wish the whole verse might burn into our hearts.

But why is this constant, persistent, sleepless, overcoming prayer so needful?

1. Why Pray? Because There Is a Devil

First of all, *because there is a devil.* He is cunning, he is mighty, he never rests, he is ever plotting the downfall of the child of God; and if the child of God relaxes in prayer, the devil will succeed in ensnaring him.

This is the thought of the context. The twelfth verse reads:

> For our wrestling is not against flesh and blood, but against the principal-ities, against the powers, against the world rulers of this darkness, against the spiritual hosts of wickedness in the heavenly places. (RV)

Then comes the 13th verse:

> Wherefore take up the whole armor of God, that ye may be able to with-stand in the evil day, and, having done all, to stand. (RV)

Next follows a description of the different parts of the Christian's armor, which we are to put on if we are to stand against the devil and his mighty wiles. Then Paul brings all to a climax in the 18th verse, telling us that to all else we must add prayer—constant, persistent, untiring, sleepless prayer in the Holy Spirit, or all else will go for nothing.

2. Prayer is God's Appointed Way to Obtain Things

A second reason for this constant, persistent, sleepless, overcoming prayer is that *prayer is God's appointed way for obtaining things, and the great secret of all lack in our experience, in our life and in our work is neglect of prayer.*

James brings this out very forcibly in the fourth chapter and second verse of his epistle: "Ye have not because ye ask not." These words contain the secret of the poverty and powerlessness of the average Christian—neglect of prayer.

"Why is it," many a Christian is asking, "I make so little progress in my Christian life?"

"Neglect of prayer," God answers. "You have not, because you ask not."

"Why is it," many a minister is asking, "I see so little fruit from my labors?"

Again God answers, "Neglect of prayer. You have not, because you ask not."

"Why is it," many a Sunday School teacher is asking, "that I see so few converted in my Sunday School class?"

Still God answers, "Neglect of prayer. You have not because you ask not."

"Why is it," both ministers and churches are asking, "that the church of Christ makes so little headway against unbelief, and error, and sin, and worldliness?"

Once more we hear God answering, "Neglect of prayer. You have not, because you ask not."

3. The Apostles Regarded Prayer as the Most Important Business of Their Lives

The third reason for this constant, persistent, sleepless, overcoming prayer is that *those men whom God set forth as a pattern of what he expected Christians to be—the apostles—regarded prayer as the most important business of their lives.*

When the multiplying responsibilities of the early church crowded in upon them, they called the multitude of the disciples unto them, and said,

> It is not reason that we should leave the Word of God, and serve tables. Wherefore, brethren, look ye out among you seven men of honest report, full of the Holy Ghost and wisdom, whom we may appoint over this business. But *we will give ourselves continually to prayer* and to the ministry of the Word. (Acts 6:2,3)

It is evident from what Paul wrote to the churches and to individuals about praying for them, that very much of his time and strength and thought was given to prayer. (Rom. 1:9 RV; Eph. 1:15,16; Col. 1:9 RV; 1 Thess. 3:10; 2 Tim. 1:3 RV)

All the mighty men of God outside the Bible have also been men of prayer. They have differed from one another in many things, but in this they have been alike.

4. Prayer Was Very Important in the Earthly Life of Jesus

But there is a still weightier reason for this constant, persistent, sleepless, overcoming prayer. It is, *prayer occupied a very prominent place and played a very important part in the earthly life of our Lord.*

Turn, for example, to Mark 1:35. We read, "And in the morning, rising up a great while before day, He went out, and departed into a solitary place, and there prayed." The preceding day had been a very busy and exciting one, but Jesus shortened the hours of needed sleep that He might arise early and give Himself to more sorely needed prayer.

Turn again to Luke 6:12, where we read, "And it came to pass in those days that He went out into a mountain to pray, and continued all night in prayer to God." Our Savior found it necessary on occasion to take a whole night for prayer.

The words "pray" and "prayer" are used at least twenty-five times in connection with our Lord in the brief record of His life in the four Gospels, and His praying is mentioned in places where the words are not used. Evidently prayer took much of the time and strength of Jesus, and a man or woman who does not spend much time in prayer, cannot properly be called a follower of Jesus Christ.

5. Praying Is the Most Important Part of the Present Ministry of Our Risen Lord

There is another reason for constant, persistent, sleepless, overcoming prayer that seems if possible even more forcible than this, namely, *praying is the most important part of the present ministry of our risen Lord.*

Christ's ministry did not close with His death. His atoning work was finished then, but when He rose and ascended to the right hand of the Father, He entered upon other work for us just as important in its place as His atoning work. It cannot be divorced from His atoning work; it rests upon that as its basis, but it is necessary to our complete salvation.

What that great present work is, by which He carries our salvation on to completeness, we read in Heb. 7:25, "Wherefore He is able also to save them to the uttermost that come unto God by Him, seeing *he ever liveth to make intercession for them.*" This verse tells us that Jesus is able to save us unto the uttermost, not merely *from* the uttermost, but *unto* the uttermost, unto entire completeness, absolute perfection, because He not merely died, but because He also "ever liveth." The verse also tells us for what purpose He now lives, "*to make intercession for us,*" to pray. Praying is the principal thing He is doing in these days. It is by His prayers that He is saving us.

The same thought is found in Paul's remarkable, triumphant challenge in Rom. 8:34—"Who is he that shall condemn? It is Christ Jesus that died, yea rather, that was raised from the dead, who is at the right hand of God, *who also maketh intercession for us.*" (RV)

If we then are to have fellowship with Jesus Christ in His present work, we must spend much time in prayer; we must give ourselves to earnest, constant, persistent, sleepless, overcoming prayer. I know of nothing that has so impressed me with a sense of the importance of praying at all seasons, being much and constantly in prayer, as the thought that that is the principal occupation at present of my risen Lord. I want to have fellowship with Him, and to that end I have asked the Father that whatever else He may make me, to make me at all events an intercessor, to make me a man who knows how to pray, and who spends much time in prayer.

This ministry of intercession is a glorious and a mighty ministry, and we can all have part in it. The man or the woman who is shut away from the public meeting by sickness can have part in it; the busy mother; the woman who has to take in washing for a living can have part—she can mingle prayers for the saints, and for her pastor, and for the unsaved, and for foreign missionaries, with the soap and water as she bends over the washtub, and not do the washing any more poorly on that account; the hard driven man of business can have part in it, praying as he hurries from duty to duty. But of course we must, if we would maintain this spirit of constant prayer, take time—and take plenty of it—when we shall shut ourselves up in the secret place alone with God for nothing but prayer.

6. Prayer Is the Way We Receive Mercy and Grace in Times of Need

The sixth reason for constant, persistent, sleepless, overcoming prayer is that *prayer is the means that God has appointed for our receiving mercy, and obtaining grace to help in time of need.*

Heb. 4:16 is one of the simplest and sweetest verses in the Bible: "Let us therefore come boldly unto the throne of grace, that we may obtain mercy, and find grace to help in time of need." These words make it very plain that God has appointed a way by which we shall seek and obtain mercy and grace. That way is prayer; bold, confident, outspoken approach to the throne of grace, the most holy place of God's presence, where our sympathizing High Priest, Jesus Christ, has entered in our behalf. (Verses 14, 15)

Mercy is what we need, grace is what we must have, or all our life and effort will end in complete failure. Prayer is the way to get them. There is infinite grace at our disposal, and we make it ours experimentally by prayer. Oh, if we only realized the fullness of God's grace, that is ours for the asking, its height and depth and length and breadth, I am sure that we would spend more time in prayer. The measure of our appropriation of grace is determined by the measure of our prayers.

Who is there that does not feel that he needs more grace? Then ask for it. Be constant and persistent in your asking. Be importunate and untiring in your asking. God delights to have us "shameless" beggars in this direction, for it shows our faith in Him, and He is mightily pleased with faith. Because of our "shamelessness" He will rise and give us as much as we need (Luke 11:8). What little streams of mercy and grace most of us know, when we might know rivers overflowing their banks!

7. Prayer in the Name of Jesus Is How We Obtain Fullness of Joy

The next reason for constant, persistent, sleepless, overcoming prayer is that *prayer in the name of Jesus Christ is the way Jesus Christ himself has appointed for his disciples to obtain fullness of joy.*

He states this simply and beautifully in John 16:24, "Hitherto have ye asked nothing in My name; ask, and ye shall receive, that your joy may be fulfilled." "Made full" is the way the Revised Version reads. Who is there that does not wish his joy filled full? Well, the way to have it filled full: is by praying in the name of Jesus. We all know people whose joy is filled full, indeed, it is just running over, is shining from their eyes, bubbling out of their very lips, and running off their finger tips when they shake hands with you. Coming in contact with them is like coming in contact with an electrical machine charged with gladness. Now people of that sort are always people that spend much time in prayer.

Why is it that prayer in the name of Christ brings such fullness of joy? In part, because we get what we ask. But that is not the only reason, nor the greatest. It makes God real. When we ask something definite of God, and He gives it, how real God becomes! He is right there! It is blessed to have a God who is real, and not merely an idea. I remember how once I was taken suddenly and seriously sick all alone in my study. I dropped upon my knees and cried to God for help. Instantly all pain left me—I was perfectly well. It seemed as if God stood right there, and had put out His hand and touched me. The joy of the healing was not so great as the joy of meeting God.

There is no greater joy on earth or in heaven, than communion with God, and prayer in the name of Jesus brings us into communion with Him. The Psalmist was surely not speaking only of future blessedness, but also of present blessedness when he said,

"In Thy presence is fullness of joy." (Ps. 16.11) O the unutterable joy of those moments when in our prayers we really press into the presence of God!

Does someone say, "I have never known any such joy as that in prayer"?

Do you take enough leisure for prayer to actually get into God's presence? Do you really give yourself up to prayer in the time which you do take?

8. Prayer Is the Way to Freedom from Worry and to God's Peace

The eighth reason for constant, persistent, sleepless, overcoming prayer is that *prayer, in every care and anxiety and need of life, with thanksgiving, is the means that God has appointed for obtaining freedom from all anxiety, and the peace of God which passeth all understanding.*

"Be careful for nothing," says Paul, "but in everything by prayer and supplication with thanksgiving let your requests be made known unto God, and the peace of God which passeth all understanding, shall keep your hearts and minds through Christ Jesus." (Phil. 4:6,7) To many this seems at the first glance, the picture of a life that is beautiful, but beyond

9

the reach of ordinary mortals; not so at all. The verse tells us how the life is attainable by every child of God: "Be careful for nothing," or as the Revised Version reads, "In nothing be anxious." The remainder of the verse tells us how, and it is very simple: "But in everything by prayer and supplication with thanksgiving let your requests be made known unto God." What could be plainer or more simple than that? Just keep in constant touch with God, and when any trouble or vexation, great or small, comes up, speak to Him about it, never forgetting to return thanks for what He has already done. What will the result be? "The peace of God which passeth all understanding shall guard your hearts and your thoughts in Christ Jesus." (RV)

That is glorious, and as simple as it is glorious! Thank God, many are trying it. Don't you know any one who is always serene? Perhaps he is a very stormy man by his natural make-up, but troubles and conflicts and reverses and bereavements may sweep around him, and the peace of God which passeth all understanding guards his heart and his thoughts in Christ Jesus.

We all know such persons. How do they manage it?

Just by prayer, that is all. Those persons who know the deep peace of God, the unfathomable peace that passeth all understanding, are always men and women of much prayer.

Some of us let the hurry of our lives crowd prayer out, and what a waste of time and energy and nerve force there is by the constant worry! One night of prayer will save us from many nights of insomnia. Time spent in prayer is not wasted, but time invested at big interest.

9. Prayer Is How We Obtain the Holy Spirit

The ninth reason for constant, persistent, sleepless, overcoming prayer is that *prayer is the method that God himself has appointed for our obtaining the Holy Spirit.*

Upon this point the Bible is very plain. Jesus says, "If ye then, being evil, know how to give good gifts unto your children, how much more shall your heavenly Father give the Holy Spirit to them that ask Him?" (Luke 11:13) Men are telling us in these days, very good men too, "You must not pray for the Holy Spirit," but what are they going to do with the plain statement of Jesus Christ, "How much more will your heavenly Father give the Holy Spirit *to them that ask Him?*"

Some years ago, when an address on the baptism with the Holy Spirit was announced, a brother came to me before the address and said with much feeling,

"Be sure and tell them not to pray for the Holy Spirit."

"I will surely not tell them that, for Jesus says, 'How much more shall your heavenly Father give the Holy Spirit to them that ask Him'."

"Oh, yes," he replied, "but that was before Pentecost."

"How about Acts 4:31? Was that before Pentecost, or after?"

"After, of course."

"Read it."

"'And when they had prayed, the place was shaken where they were assembled together; and they were all *filled with the Holy Ghost,* and they spake the Word of God with boldness.'"

"How about Acts 8:15? Was that before Pentecost or after?"

"After."

"Please read."

"'Who, when they were come down, *prayed* for them, that they might receive the Holy Ghost.'"

He made no answer. What could he answer? It is plain as day in the Word of God that before Pentecost and after, the first baptism and the subsequent fillings with the Holy Spirit were received in answer to definite prayer. Experience also teaches this.

Doubtless many have received the Holy Spirit the moment of their surrender to God, before there was time to pray, but how many there are who know that their first definite baptism with the Holy Spirit came while they were on their knees or faces before God, alone or in company with others, and who again and again since that have been filled with the Holy Spirit in the place of prayer!

I know this as definitely as I know that my thirst has been quenched while I was drinking water. Early one morning in the Chicago Avenue Church prayer room, where several hundred people had been assembled a number of hours in prayer, the Holy Spirit fell so manifestly, and the whole place was so filled with His presence, that no one could speak or pray, but

11

sobs of joy filled the place. Men went out of that room to different parts of the country, taking trains that very morning, and reports soon came back of the out pouring of God's Holy Spirit in answer to prayer. Others went out into the city with the blessing of God upon them. This is only one instance among many that might be cited from personal experience.

If we would only spend more time in prayer, there would be more fullness of the Spirit's power in our work. Many and many a man who once worked unmistakably in the power of the Holy Spirit is now filling the air with empty shoutings, and beating it with his meaningless gesticulations, because he has let prayer be crowded out. We must spend much time on our knees before God, if we are to continue in the power of the Holy Spirit.

10. Prayer Protects Us from Temptation and Prepares Us for Jesus' Return

The tenth reason for constant, persistent, sleepless, overcoming prayer is that *prayer is the means that Christ has appointed whereby our hearts shall not become overcharged with surfeiting and drunkenness and cares of this life, and so the day of Christ's return come upon us suddenly as a snare.*

One of the most interesting and solemn passages upon prayer in the Bible is along this line. (Luke 21:34–36)

> Take heed to yourselves, lest at any time your hearts be overcharged with surfeiting and drunkenness and cares of this life, and so that day come upon you unawares. For as a snare shall it come on all them that dwell in the face of the whole earth. Watch ye therefore, and *pray always*, that ye may be accounted worthy to escape all these things that shall come to pass, and to stand before the Son of man.

According to this passage there is only one way in which we can be prepared for the coming of the Lord when He appears, that is, through much prayer.

The coming again of Jesus Christ is a subject that is awakening much interest and much discussion in our day; but it is one thing to be interested in the Lord's return, and to talk about it, and quite another thing to be prepared for it. We live in an atmosphere that has a constant tendency to unfit us for Christ's coming. The world tends to draw us down by its gratifications and by its cares. There is only one way by which we can rise triumphant above these things—by constant watching unto prayer, that is, by sleeplessness unto prayer. "Watch" in this passage is the same strong word used in Eph. 6:18, and "always" the same strong phrase "in every season." The man who spends little time in prayer, who is not steadfast and constant in prayer, will not be ready for the Lord when He comes. But we may be ready. How? Pray! Pray! Pray!

11. Because of What Prayer Accomplishes

There is one more reason for constant, persistent, sleepless, overcoming prayer, and it is a mighty one: *because of what prayer accomplishes*. Much has really been said upon that already, but there is much also that should be added.

> A. *Prayer promotes our spiritual growth as almost nothing else, indeed as nothing else but Bible study; and true prayer and true Bible study go hand in hand.*

It is through prayer that my sin is brought to light, my most hidden sin. As I kneel before God and pray, "Search me, O God, and know my heart; try me, and know my thoughts; and see if there be any wicked way in me," (Ps.139:23,24), God shoots the penetrating rays of His light into the innermost recesses of my heart, and the sins I never suspected are brought to view. In answer to prayer, God washes me from mine iniquity and cleanses me from my sin. (Ps. 51:2) In answer to prayer, my eyes are opened to behold wondrous things out of God's Word. (Ps. 119:18) In answer to prayer I get wisdom to know God's way (Jas. 1:5) and strength to walk in it. As I meet God in prayer and gaze into His face, I am changed into His own image from glory to glory. (2 Cor. 3:18) Each day of true prayer life finds me more like my glorious Lord.

John Welch, son-in-law to John Knox, was one of the most faithful men of prayer this world ever saw. He counted that day ill spent in which seven or eight hours were not used alone with God in prayer and the study of His Word. An old man, speaking of him after his death, said, "He was a type of Christ."

How came he to be so like his Master?

His prayer life explains the mystery.

B. *Prayer brings power into our work.*

If we wish power for any work to which God calls us, be it preaching, teaching, personal work, or the rearing of our children, we can get it by earnest prayer.

A woman with a little boy who was perfectly incorrigible once came to me in desperation and said:

"What shall I do with him?"

I asked, "Have you ever tried prayer?"

She said that she had prayed for him, she thought. I asked if she had made his conversion and his character a matter of definite, expectant prayer. She replied that she had not been definite in the matter. She began that day, and at once there was a marked change in the child, and he grew up into Christian manhood.

How many a Sunday School teacher has taught for months and years, and seen no real fruit from his labors, and then has learned the secret of intercession, and by earnest pleading with God, has seen his scholars brought one by one to Christ! How many a poor preacher has become a mighty man of God by casting away his confidence in his own ability and gifts, and giving himself up to God to wait upon Him for the power that comes from on high! John Livingstone spent a night, with some others like-minded, in prayer to God and religious conversation, and when he preached next day in the Kirk of Shotts, five hundred people were converted, or dated some definite uplift in their life to that occasion. Prayer and power are inseparable.

C. *Prayer avails for the conversion of others.*

There are few converted in this world unless in connection with someone's prayers. I formerly thought that no human being had anything to do with my own conversion, for I was not converted in church or Sunday school, or in personal conversation with any one. I was awakened in the middle of the night and converted. As far as I can remember I had not the slightest thought of being converted, or of anything of that character, when I went to bed and fell asleep; but I was awakened in the middle of the night and converted probably inside of five minutes. A few minutes before, I was about as near eternal perdition as one gets. I had one foot over the brink and was trying to get the other one over. I say I thought no human being had anything to do with it, but I had forgotten my mother's prayers, and I afterward learned that one of my college classmates had chosen me as one to pray for until I was saved.

Prayer often avails where everything else fails. How utterly all of Monica's efforts and entreaties failed with her son, but her prayers prevailed with God, and the dissolute youth became St. Augustine, the mighty man of God. By prayer the bitterest enemies of the Gospel have become its most valiant defenders, the greatest scoundrels the truest sons of God, and the vilest women, the purest saints. Oh, the power of prayer to reach down, down, down, where hope itself seems vain, and lift men and women up, up, up into fellowship with and likeness to God. It is simply wonderful! How little we appreciate this marvelous weapon!

D. Prayer brings blessings to the church.

The history of the church has always been a history of grave difficulties to overcome. The devil hates the church and seeks in every way to block its progress; now by false doctrine, again by division, again by inward corruption of life. But by prayer, a clear way can be made through everything. Prayer will root out heresy, allay misunderstanding, sweep away jealousies and animosities, obliterate immoralities, and bring in the full tide of God's reviving grace. History abundantly proves this. In the hour of darkest portent, when the case of the church, local or universal, has seemed beyond hope, believing men and believing women have met together and cried to God and the answer has come.

It was so in the days of Knox, it was so in the days of Wesley and Whitfield, it was so in the days of Edwards and Brainerd, it was so in the days of Finney, it was so in the days of the great revival of 1857 in this country and of 1859 in Ireland, and it will be so again in your day and mine. Satan has marshaled his forces. Christian science with its false Christ—a woman—lifts high its head. Others making great pretensions of apostolic methods, but covering the rankest dishonesty and hypocrisy with these pretensions, speak with loud assurance. Christians equally loyal to the great fundamental truths of the Gospel are glowering at one another with a devil-sent suspicion. The world, the flesh, and the devil are holding high carnival. It is now a dark day, *but*—now "it is time for Thee, Lord, to work;

for they have made void Thy law." (Ps. 119:126) And He is getting ready to work, and now He is listening for the voice of prayer. Will He hear it? Will He hear it from you? Will He hear it from the church as a body? I believe He will.

Chapter 2

Praying Unto God

We have seen something of the tremendous importance and the re-sistless power of prayer, and now we come directly to the question—how to pray with power.

1. Pray *to* God

In the twelfth chapter of the Acts of the Apostles we have the record of a prayer that prevailed with God, and brought to pass great results. In the fifth verse of this chapter, the manner and method of this prayer is described in few words: "Prayer was made without ceasing of the church *unto God* for him."

The first thing to notice in this verse is the brief expression "unto God." The prayer that has power is the prayer that is offered unto God.

But some will say, "Is not all prayer unto God?"

No. Very much of so-called prayer, both public and private, is not unto God. In order that a prayer should be really unto God, there must be a definite and conscious approach to God when we pray; we must have a definite and vivid realization that God is bending over us and listening as we pray. In very much of our prayer there is really but little thought of God. Our mind is taken up with the thought of what we need, and is not occupied with the thought of the mighty and loving Father of whom we are seeking it. Oftentimes it is the case that we are occupied neither with the need nor with the One to whom we are praying, but our mind is wandering here and there throughout the world. There is no power in that sort of prayer. But when we really come into God's presence, really meet Him face to face in the place of prayer, really seek the things that we desire *from Him,* then there is power.

If, then, we would pray aright, the first thing that we should do is to see to it that we really get an audience with God, that we really get into His very presence. Before a word of petition is offered, we should have the definite and vivid consciousness that we are talking to God, and should believe that He is listening to our petition and is going to grant the thing that we ask of Him. This is only possible by the Holy Spirit's power, so we should look to the Holy Spirit to really lead us into the presence of God, and should not be hasty in words until He has actually brought us there.

One night a very active Christian man dropped into a little prayer meeting that I was leading. Before we knelt to pray, I said something like the above, telling all the friends to be sure before they prayed, and while they were praying, that they really were in God's presence, that they had the thought of Him definitely in mind, and to be more taken up with Him than with their petition. A few days after I met this same gentleman, and he said that this simple thought was entirely new to him, that it had made prayer an entirely new experience to him.

If then we would pray aright, these two little words must sink deep into our hearts, *"unto God."*

2. Pray Intensely

The second secret of effective praying is found in the same verse, in the words *"without ceasing."*

In the Revised Version, "without ceasing" is rendered "earnestly." Neither rendering gives the full force of the Greek. The word means literally "stretched-out-ed-ly." It is a pictorial word, and wonderfully expressive. It

18

represents the soul on a stretch of earnest and intense desire. "Intensely" would perhaps come as near translating it as any English word. It is the word used of our Lord in Luke 22:44 where it is said, "He prayed more earnestly: and His sweat was as it were great drops of blood falling down to the ground."

We read in Heb. 5:7 that "in the days of His flesh" Christ "offered up prayers and supplications with strong crying and tears." In Rom. 15:30, Paul beseeches the saints in Rome to *strive* together with him in their prayers. The word translated "strive" means primarily to contend, as in athletic games or in a fight. In other words, the prayer that prevails with God is the prayer into which we put our whole soul, stretching out toward God in intense and agonizing desire. Much of our modern prayer has no power in it because there is no heart in it. We rush into God's presence, run through a string of petitions, jump up, and go out. If someone should ask us an hour afterward for what we prayed, oftentimes we could not tell. If we put so little heart into our prayers, we cannot expect God to put much heart into answering them.

We hear much in our day of the rest of faith, but there is such a thing as the fight of faith in prayer as well as in effort. Those who would have us think that they have attained to some sublime height of faith and trust because they never know any agony of conflict or of prayer, have surely gotten beyond their Lord, and beyond the mightiest victors for God, both in effort and prayer, that the ages of Christian history have known. When we learn to come to God with an intensity of desire that wrings the soul, then shall we know a power in prayer that most of us do not know now.

But how shall we attain to this earnestness in prayer?

Not by trying to work ourselves up into it. The true method is explained in Rom. 8:26, "And in like manner the Spirit also helpeth our infirmity: for we know not how to pray as we ought; but the Spirit Himself maketh intercession for us with groanings which cannot be uttered." (RV) The earnestness that we work up in the energy of the flesh is a repulsive thing. The earnestness wrought in us by the power of the Holy Spirit is pleasing to God. Here again, if we would pray aright, we must look to the Spirit of God to teach us to pray.

It is in this connection that fasting comes. In Dan. 9:3 we read that Daniel set his face "unto the Lord God, to seek by prayer and supplications, with fasting, and sackcloth, and ashes." There are those who think that fasting belongs to the old dispensation; but when we look at Acts 14:23, and Acts 13:2,3, we find that it was practiced by the earnest men of the apostolic day.

If we would pray with power, we should pray with fasting. This of course does not mean that we should fast every time we pray; but there are times of emergency or special crisis in work or in our individual lives, when men of downright earnestness will withdraw themselves even from the gratification of natural appetites that would be perfectly proper under other circumstances, that they may give themselves up wholly to prayer. There is a peculiar power in such prayer. Every great crisis in life and work should be met in that way. There is nothing pleasing to God in our giving up in a purely Pharisaic and legal way things which are pleasant, but there is power in that downright earnestness and determination to obtain in prayer the things of which we sorely feel our need, that leads us to put away everything, even the things in themselves most right and necessary, that we may set our faces to find God, and obtain blessings from Him.

3. The Power of United Prayer

A third secret of right praying is also found in this same verse, Acts 12:5. It appears in the three words *"of the church."*

There is power in *united prayer*. Of course there is power in the prayer of an individual, but there is vastly increased power in united prayer. God delights in the unity of His people, and seeks to emphasize it in every way, and so He pronounces a special blessing upon united prayer. We read in Matt. 18:19, "If two of you shall agree on earth as touching anything that they shall ask, it shall be done for them of My Father which is in heaven." This unity, however, must be real. The passage just quoted does not say that if two shall agree in asking, but if two shall agree *as touching* anything they shall ask. Two persons might agree to ask for the same thing, and yet there be no real agreement as touching the thing they asked. One might ask it because he really desired it, the other might ask it simply to please his friend. But where there is real agreement, where the Spirit of God brings two believers into perfect harmony as concerning that which they may ask of God, where the Spirit lays the same burden on two hearts; in all such prayer there is absolutely irresistible power.

Chapter 3

Obeying and Praying

1. Obtaining What We Ask

One of the most significant verses in the Bible on prayer is 1 John 3:22. John says, "And whatsoever we ask, we receive of Him, because we keep His commandments, and do those things that are pleasing in His sight."

What an astounding statement! John says in so many words, that everything he asked for he got. How many of us can say this: "Whatsoever I ask I receive"? But John explains why this was so, "Because we keep His commandments, and do those things that are pleasing in His sight." In other words, the one who expects God to do as he asks Him, must on his part *do whatever God bids Him.* If we give a listening ear to all God's commands to us, He will give a listening ear to all our petitions to Him. If, on the other hand, we turn a deaf ear to His precepts, He will be likely to turn a deaf ear to our prayers. Here we find the secret of much unanswered prayer. We are not listening to God's Word, and therefore He is not listening to our petitions.

I was once speaking to a woman who had been a professed Christian, but had given it all up. I asked her why she was not a Christian still. She replied, because she did not believe the Bible. I asked her why she did not believe the Bible.

"Because I have tried its promises and found them untrue."

"Which promises?"

"The promises about prayer."

"Which promises about prayer?"

"Does it not say in the Bible, 'Whatsoever ye ask believing ye shall receive'?"

"It says something nearly like that."

"Well, I asked fully expecting to get and did not receive, so the promise failed."

"Was the promise made to you?"

"Why, certainly, it is made to all Christians, is it not?"

"No, God carefully defines who the 'ye's' are, whose believing prayers He agrees to answer."

I then turned her to 1 John 3:22, and read the description of those whose prayers had power with God.

"Now," I said, "were you keeping His commandments and doing those things which are pleasing in His sight?"

She frankly confessed that she was not, and soon came to see that the real difficulty was not with God's promises, but with herself. That is the difficulty with many an unanswered prayer today: the one who offers it is not obedient.

If we would have power in prayer, we must be earnest students of His Word to find out what His will regarding us is, and then having found it, do it. One unconfessed act of disobedience on our part will shut the ear of God against many petitions.

2. Pleasing God

But this verse goes beyond the mere keeping of God's commandments. John tells us that we must *do those things that are pleasing in His sight*.

There are many things which it would be pleasing to God for us to do which He has not specifically commanded us. A true child is not content with

24

merely doing those things which his father specifically commands him to do. He studies to know his father's will, and if he thinks that there is any thing that he can do that would please his father, he does it gladly, though his father has never given him any specific order to do it. So it is with the true child of God. He does not ask merely whether certain things are commanded or certain things forbidden. He studies to know his Father's will in all things.

There are many Christians today who are doing things that are not pleasing to God, and leaving undone things which would be pleasing to God. When you speak to them about these things they will confront you at once with the question, "Is there any command in the Bible not to do this thing?" And if you cannot show them some verse in which the matter in question is plainly forbidden, they think they are under no obligation whatever to give it up; but a true child of God does not demand a specific command. If we make it our study to find out and to do the things which are pleasing to God, He will make His study to do the things which are pleasing to us. Here again we find the explanation of much unanswered prayer: we are not making it the study of our lives to know what would please our Father, and so our prayers are not answered.

Take as an illustration of questions that are constantly coming up, the matter of theater going, dancing and the use of tobacco. Many who are indulging in these things will ask you triumphantly if you speak against them, "Does the Bible say, 'Thou shalt not go to the theater'?" "Does the Bible say, 'Thou shalt not dance'?" "Does the Bible say, 'Thou shalt not smoke'?" That is not the question. The question is, "Is our heavenly Father well pleased when He sees one of His children in the theater, at the dance, or smoking?" That is a question for each to decide for himself, prayerfully, seeking light from the Holy Spirit. "Where is the harm in these things?" many ask. It is aside from our purpose to go into the general question, but beyond a doubt there is this great harm in many a case; they rob our prayers of power.

3. Pray "In Truth"

Psalm 145:18 throws a great deal of light on the question of how to pray: "The Lord is nigh unto all them that call upon Him, to all that call upon Him in truth."

25

That little expression "in truth" is worthy of study. If you will take your concordance and go through the Bible, you will find that this expression means "in reality,"; "in sincerity." The prayer that God answers is the prayer that is real, the prayer that asks for something that is sincerely desired.

Much prayer is insincere. People ask for things which they do not wish. Many a woman is praying for the conversion of her husband, who does not really wish her husband to be converted. She thinks that she does, but if she knew what would be involved in the conversion of her husband, how it would necessitate an entire revolution in his manner of doing business, and how consequently it would reduce their income and make necessary an entire change in their method of living, the real prayer of her heart would be, if she were to be sincere with God:

"O God, do not convert my husband."

She does not wish his conversion at so great cost.

Many a church is praying for a revival that does not really desire a revival. They think they do, for to their minds a revival means an increase of membership, an increase of income, an increase of reputation among the churches, but if they knew what a real revival meant, what a searching of hearts on the part of professed Christians would be involved, what a radical transformation of individual, domestic and social life would be brought about, and many other things that would come to pass if the Spirit of God was poured out in reality and power; if all this were known, the real cry of the church would be:

"O God, keep us from having a revival."

Many a minister is praying for the baptism with the Holy Spirit who does not really desire it. He thinks he does, for the baptism with the Spirit means to him new joy, new power in preaching the Word, a wider reputation among men, a larger prominence in the church of Christ. But if he understood what a baptism with the Holy Spirit really involved, how for example it would necessarily bring him into antagonism with the world, and with unspiritual Christians, how it would cause his name to be "cast out as evil," how it might necessitate his leaving a good comfortable living and going down to work in the slums, or even in some foreign land; if he understood all this, his prayer quite likely would be—if he were to express the real wish of his heart:

"O God, save me from being baptized with the Holy Ghost."

But when we do come to the place where we really desire the conversion of friends at any cost, really desire the outpouring of the Holy Spirit whatever it may involve, really desire the baptism with the Holy Ghost come what may, where we desire anything "in truth" and then call upon God for it "in truth," God is going to hear.

CHAPTER 4

Praying in the Name of Christ and According to the Will of God

1. Asking in Jesus' Name

It was a wonderful word about prayer that Jesus spoke to His disciples on the night before His crucifixion, "Whatsoever ye shall ask *in My name,* that will I do, that the Father may be glorified in the Son. If ye shall ask anything in My name, I will do it."

Prayer in the name of Christ has power with God. God is well pleased with His Son Jesus Christ. He hears Him always, and He also hears always the prayer that is really in His name. There is a fragrance in the name of Christ that makes acceptable to God every prayer that bears it.

But what is it to pray in the name of Christ?

Many explanations have been attempted that to ordinary minds do not explain. But there is nothing mystical or mysterious about this expression. If one will go through the Bible and examine all the passages in which the expression "in My name" or "in His name" or synonymous expressions are used, he will find that it means just about what it does in modern usage. If I go to a bank and hand in a check with my name signed to it, I ask of that bank *in my own name.* If I have money deposited in that bank, the check will be cashed; if not, it will not be. If, however, I go to a bank with some-body else's name signed to the check, I am asking *in his name,* and it does not matter whether I have money in that bank or any other, if the person whose name is signed to the check has money there, the check will be cashed.

If, for example, I should go to the First National Bank of Chicago, and pres-ent a check which I had signed for $50.00, the paying teller would say to me:

"Why, Mr. Torrey, we cannot cash that. You have no money in this bank."

But if I should go to the First National Bank with a check for $5,000.00 made payable to me, and signed by one of the large depositors in that bank, they would not ask whether I had money in that bank or in any bank, but would honor the check at once.

So it is when I go to the bank of heaven, when I go to God in prayer. I have nothing deposited there, I have absolutely no credit there, and if I go in my own name I will get absolutely nothing; but Jesus Christ has unlim-ited credit in heaven, and He has granted to me the privilege of going to the bank with His name on my checks, and when I thus go, my prayers will be honored to any extent.

To pray then in the name of Christ is to pray on the ground, not of my credit, but His; to renounce the thought that I have any claims on God whatever, and approach Him on the ground of God's claims. Praying in the name of Christ is not merely adding the phrase "I ask these things in Jesus' name" to my prayer. I may put that phrase in my prayer and really be resting in my own merit all the time. But when I really do approach God, not on the ground of my merit, but on the ground of Christ's merit, not on the ground of my goodness, but on the ground of the atoning blood (Heb. 10:19), God will hear me. Very much of our modern prayer is vain because men approach God imagining that they have some claim upon God whereby He is under obligations to answer their prayers.

Years ago when Mr. Moody was young in Christian work, he visited a town in Illinois. A judge in the town was an infidel. This judge's wife be-sought Mr. Moody to call upon her husband, but Mr. Moody replied:

"I cannot talk with your husband. I am only an uneducated young Christian, and your husband is a book infidel."

But the wife would not take no for an answer, so Mr. Moody made the call. The clerks in the outer office tittered as the young salesman from Chicago went in to talk with the scholarly judge.

The conversation was short. Mr. Moody said:

"Judge, I can't talk with you. You are a book infidel, and I have no learning, but I simply want to say if you are ever converted, I want you to let me know."

The judge replied: "Yes, young man, if I am ever converted I will let you know. Yes, I will let you know."

The conversation ended. The clerks tittered still louder when the zealous young Christian left the office, but the judge was converted within a year. Mr. Moody, visiting the town again, asked the judge to explain how it came about. The judge said:

"One night, when my wife was at prayer meeting, I began to grow very uneasy and miserable. I did not know what was the matter with me, but finally retired before my wife come home. I could not sleep all that night. I got up early, told my wife that I would eat no breakfast, and went down to the office. I told the clerks they could take a holiday, and shut myself up in the inner office. I kept growing more and more miserable, and finally I got down and asked God to forgive my sins, but I would not say 'for Jesus' sake,' for I was a Unitarian and I did not believe in the atonement. I kept praying 'God forgive my sins'; but no answer came. At last in desperation I cried, 'O God, for Christ's sake forgive my sins,' and found peace at once."

The judge had no access to God until he came in the name of Christ, but when he thus came, he was heard and answered at once.

2. Ask According to God's Will

Great light is thrown upon the subject "How to Pray" by 1 John 5:14,15:

> And this is the boldness which we have toward Him, that if we ask anything *according to his will*, He heareth us; and if we know that He heareth us whatsoever we ask, we know that we have the petitions which we have asked of Him. (RV)

This passage teaches us plainly that if we are to pray aright, we must pray according to God's will, then will we beyond a peradventure [doubt] get the thing we ask of Him.

But can we know the will of God? Can we know that any specific prayer is according to His will?

We most surely can.

How?

A. First by the Word. God has revealed His will in His Word.

When anything is definitely promised in the Word of God, we know that it is His will to give that thing. If then when I pray, I can find some definite promise of God's Word and lay that promise before God, I know that He hears me, and if I know that He hears me, I know that I have the petition that I have asked of Him. For example, when I pray for wisdom I know that it is the will of God to give me wisdom, for He says so in James 1:5: "If any of you lack wisdom, let him ask of God, that giveth to all men liberally, and upbraideth not; and it shall be given him." So when I ask for wisdom I know that the prayer is heard, and that wisdom will be given me. In like manner, when I pray for the Holy Spirit I know from Luke 11:13 that it is God's will, that my prayer is heard, and that I have the petition that I have asked of Him: "If ye then, being evil, know how to give good gifts unto your children, how much more shall your heavenly Father give the Holy Spirit to them that ask Him?"

Some years ago a minister came to me at the close of an address on prayer at a Y.M.C.A. Bible school, and said,

"You have produced upon those young men the impression that they can ask for definite things and get the very things that they ask."

I replied that I did not know whether that was the impression that I produced or not, but that was certainly the impression that I desired to produce.

"But," he replied, "that is not right. We cannot be sure, for we don't know God's will."

I turned him at once to James 1:5, read it, and said to him,

"Is it not God's will to give us wisdom, and if you ask for wisdom do you not know that you are going to get it?"

"Ah!" he said, "we don't know what wisdom is."

I said, "No, if we did, we would not need to ask; but whatever wisdom may be, don't you know that you will get it?"

Certainly it is our privilege to know. When we have a specific promise in the Word of God, if we doubt that it is God's will, or if we doubt that God will do the thing that we ask, we make God a liar.

Here is one of the greatest secrets of prevailing prayer: to study the Word to find what God's will is, as revealed there in the promises, and then simply take these promises and spread them out before God in prayer, with the absolutely unwavering expectation that He will do what He has promised in His Word.

B. But there is still another way in which we may know the will of God, that is, by the teaching of His Holy Spirit.

There are many things that we need from God which are not covered by any specific promise, but we are not left in ignorance of the will of God even then. In Rom. 8:26,27 we are told:

> And in like manner the Spirit also helpeth our infirmity: for we know not how to pray as we ought; but the Spirit Himself maketh intercession for us with groanings which cannot be uttered; and He that searcheth the hearts knoweth what is the mind of the spirit, because He maketh intercession for the saints *according to the will of God.* (RV)

Here we are distinctly told that the Spirit of God prays in us, draws out our prayer, in the line of God's will. When we are thus led out by the Holy Spirit in any direction, to pray for any given object, we may do it in all confidence that it is God's will, and that we are to get the very thing we ask of Him, even though there is no specific promise to cover the case. Often God by His Spirit lays upon us a heavy burden of prayer for some given individual. We cannot rest, we pray for him with groanings which cannot be uttered. Perhaps the man is entirely beyond our reach, but God hears the prayer, and in many a case it is not long before we hear of his definite conversion.

The passage 1 John 5:14,15 is one of the most abused passages in the Bible: "This is *the confidence* that we have in Him, that, if we ask anything according to His will, He heareth us; and if we know that He hear us, whatsoever we ask, we know that we have the petitions that we desired of Him." The Holy Spirit beyond a doubt put it into the Bible to encourage our faith. It begins with "This is *the confidence* that we have in Him," and closes with *"we know* that we have the petitions that we desired of Him;" but one of the most frequent usages of this passage, which was so manifestly given to beget confidence, is to introduce an element of uncertainty into our prayers. Oftentimes when one waxes confident in prayer, some cautious brother will come and say:

"Now, don't be too confident. If it is God's will He will do it. You should put in, 'If it be Thy will.'"

Doubtless there are many times when we do not know the will of God, and in all prayer submission to the excellent will of God should underlie it; but when we know God's will, there need be no "ifs"; and this passage was not put into the Bible in order that we might introduce "ifs" into all our prayers, but in order that we might throw our "ifs" to the wind, and have *"confidence"* and *"know* that we have the petitions which we have asked of Him."

CHAPTER 5

Praying in the Spirit

1. "In The Spirit"

Over and over again in what has already been said, we have seen our dependence upon the Holy Spirit in prayer. This comes out very definitely in Eph. 6:18, "Praying always with all prayer and supplication *in the Spirit,*" and in Jude 20, "Praying *in the Holy Ghost.*" Indeed the whole secret of prayer is found in these three words, "in the Spirit." It is the prayer that God the Holy Spirit inspires that God the Father answers.

The disciples did not know how to pray as they ought, so they came to Jesus and said, "Lord, teach us to pray." We know not how to pray as we ought, but we have another Teacher and Guide right at hand to help us (John 14:16,17), "The Spirit helpeth our infirmity" (Rom. 8:26 RV). He teaches us how to pray. True prayer is prayer in the Spirit; that is, the prayer the Spirit inspires and directs. When we come into God's presence we should recognize "our infirmity"; our ignorance of what we should pray for or how we should pray for it, and in the consciousness of our utter inability to pray aright we should look up to the Holy Spirit, casting ourselves

35

utterly upon Him to direct our prayers, to lead out our desires and to guide our utterance of them.

Nothing can be more foolish in prayer than to rush heedlessly into God's presence, and ask the first thing that comes into our mind, or that some thoughtless friend has asked us to pray for. When we first come into God's presence we should be silent before Him. We should look up to Him to send His Holy Spirit to teach us how to pray. We must wait for the Holy Spirit, and surrender ourselves to the Spirit, then we shall pray aright.

Oftentimes when we come to God in prayer, we do not feel like praying. What shall one do in such a case? Cease praying until he does feel like it? Not at all. When we feel least like praying is the time when we most need to pray. We should wait quietly before God and tell Him how cold and prayerless our hearts are, and look up to Him and trust Him and expect Him to send the Holy Spirit to warm our hearts and draw them out in prayer. It will not be long before the glow of the Spirit's presence will fill our hearts, and we will begin to pray with freedom, directness, earnestness, and power. Many of the most blessed seasons of prayer I have ever known have begun with a feeling of utter deadness and prayerlessness, but in my helplessness and coldness I have cast myself upon God, and looked to Him to send His Holy Spirit to teach me to pray, and He has done it.

When we pray in the Spirit, we will pray for the right things and in the right way. There will be joy and power in our prayer.

2. With Faith

If we are to pray with power, we must pray *with faith*. In Mark 11:24 Jesus says, "Therefore I say unto you, What things soever ye desire, when ye pray, believe that ye receive them, and ye shall have them." No matter how positive any promise of God's Word may be, we will not enjoy it in actual experience unless we confidently expect its fulfillment in answer to our prayer. "If any of you lack wisdom," says James, "let him ask of God that giveth to all men liberally, and upbraideth not; and it shall be given him." Now that promise is as positive as a promise can be, but the next verse adds,

> But let him ask in faith, nothing doubting: for he that doubteth is like the surge of the sea driven by the wind and tossed. For let not that man think that he shall receive anything of the Lord. (RV)

There must then be confident unwavering expectation. But there is a faith that goes beyond expectation, that believes that the prayer is heard and the promise granted. This comes out in the Revised Version of Mark 11:24, "Therefore I say unto you, All things whatsoever ye pray and ask for, believe that ye *have* received them, and ye shall have them."

But how can one get this faith?

Let us say with all emphasis, it cannot be pumped up. Many a one reads this promise about the prayer of faith, and then asks for things that he desires and tries to make himself believe that God has heard the prayer. This ends only in disappointment, for it is not real faith and the thing is not granted. It is at this point that many people make a collapse of faith altogether by trying to work up faith by an effort of their will, and as the thing they made themselves believe they expected to get is not given, the very foundation of faith is oftentimes undermined.

But how does real faith come?

Rom 10:17 answers the question: "So then faith cometh by hearing, and hearing *by the Word of* God." If we are to have real faith, we must study the Word of God and find out what is promised, then simply believe the promises of God. Faith must have a warrant. Trying to believe something that you want to believe is not faith. Believing what God says in His Word is faith. If I am to have faith when I pray, I must find some promise in the Word of God on which to rest my faith. Faith furthermore comes through the Spirit. The Spirit knows the will of God, and if I pray in the Spirit, and look to the Spirit to teach me God's will, He will lead me out in prayer along the line of that will, and give me faith that the prayer is to be answered; but in no case does real faith come by simply determining that you are going to get the thing that you want to get.

If there is no promise in the Word of God, and no clear leading of the Spirit, there can be no real faith, and there should be no upbraiding of self for lack of faith in such a case. But if the thing desired is promised in the Word of God, we may well upbraid ourselves for lack of faith if we doubt; for we are making God a liar by doubting His Word.

CHAPTER 6

Always Praying and Not Fainting

In two parables in the Gospel of Luke, Jesus teaches with great emphasis the lesson that men ought always to pray and not to faint. The first parable is found in Luke 11:5–8, and the other in Luke 18:1–8.

> And He said unto them, Which of you shall have a friend, and shall go unto him at midnight, and say unto him: "Friend, lend me three loaves; for a friend of mine in his journey is come to me, and I have nothing to set before him?" And he from within shall answer and say: "Trouble me not: the door is now shut, and my children are with me in bed. I cannot rise and give thee." I say unto you, Though he will not rise and give him because he is his friend, yet because of his importunity he will rise and give him as many as he needeth. (Luke 11:5–8)

> . . .And He spake a parable unto them to this end, that men always ought to pray and not to faint, saying: There was in a city a judge which feared not God, neither regarded man; and there was a widow in that city; and she came to him, saying:

> "Avenge me of mine adversary."

And he would not for a while; but afterward he said within himself: "Though I fear not God, nor regard man, yet because this widow troubleth me I will avenge her, lest by her continual coming she weary me."

And the Lord said, "Hear what the unjust judge saith. And shall not God avenge his own elect, which cry day and night unto Him, though He bear long with them? I tell you that He will avenge them speedily. Nevertheless, when the Son of Man cometh, shall He find faith on the earth?" (Luke 18:1–8)

In the former of these two parables Jesus sets forth the necessity of importunity in prayer in a startling way. The word rendered "importunity" means literally "shamelessness," as if Jesus would have us understand that God would have us draw nigh to Him with a determination to obtain the things we seek that will not be put to shame by any seeming refusal or delay on God's part. God delights in the holy boldness that will not take "no" for an answer. It is an expression of great faith, and nothing pleases God more than faith.

Jesus seemed to put the Syro-Phoenician woman away almost with rudeness, but she would not be put away, and Jesus looked upon her shameless importunity with pleasure, and said, "O woman, great is thy faith; be it unto thee even as thou wilt." (Matt. 15:28) God does not always let us get things at our first effort. He would train us and make us strong men by compelling us to work hard for the best things. So also He does not always give us what we ask in answer to the first prayer; He would train us and make us strong men of prayer by compelling us to pray hard for the best things. He makes us *pray through*.

I am glad that this is so. There is no more blessed training in prayer than that that comes through being compelled to ask again and again and again even through a long period of years before one obtains that which he seeks from God. Many people call it submission to the will of God when God does not grant them their requests at the first or second asking, and they say:

"Well, perhaps it is not God's will."

As a rule this is not submission, but spiritual laziness. We do not call it submission to the will of God when we give up after one or two efforts to obtain things by action; we call it lack of strength of character. When the

40

strong man of action starts out to accomplish a thing, if he does not accomplish it the first, or second or one hundredth time, he keeps hammering away until he does accomplish it; and the strong man of prayer when he starts to pray for a thing keeps on praying until he prays it through, and obtains what he seeks. We should be careful about what we ask from God, but when we do begin to pray for a thing we should never give up praying for it until we get it, or until God makes it very clear and very definite to us that it is not His will to give it.

Some would have us believe that it shows unbelief to pray twice for the same thing, that we ought to "take it" the first time that we ask. Doubtless there are times when we are able through faith in the Word or the leading of the Holy Spirit to *claim* the first time that which we have asked of God; but beyond question there are other times when we must pray again and again and again for the same thing before we get our answer. Those who have gotten beyond praying twice for the same thing have gotten beyond their Master. (Matt. 26:44) George Muller prayed for two men daily for upwards of sixty years. One of these men was converted shortly before his death, I think at the last service that George Muller held; the other was converted within a year after his death. One of the great needs of the present day is men and women who will not only start out to pray for things, but pray on and on and on until they obtain that which they seek from the Lord.

CHAPTER 7

Abiding in Christ

"If ye abide in Me, and My words abide in you, ye shall ask what ye will, and it shall be done unto you." (John 15:7) The whole secret of prayer is found in these words of our Lord. Here is prayer that has unbounded power: "Ask *what ye will,* and it shall be done unto you."

There is a way then of asking and getting precisely what we ask and getting all we ask. Christ gives two conditions of this all-prevailing prayer.

1. "Abide in Me"

The first condition is, "If ye abide in Me."

What is it to abide in Christ?

Some explanations that have been given of this are so mystical or so profound that to many simple-minded children of God they mean practically nothing at all; but what Jesus meant was really very simple.

He had been comparing Himself to a vine, His disciples to the branches in the vine. Some branches continued in the vine, that is, remained in living union with the vine, so that the sap or life of the vine constantly flowed into these branches. They had no independent life of their own. Everything in them was simply the outcome of the life of the vine flowing into them. Their buds, their leaves, their blossoms, their fruit, were really not theirs, but the buds, leaves, blossoms and fruit of the vine. Other branches were completely severed from the vine, or else the flow of the sap or life of the vine into them was in some way hindered. Now for us to abide in Christ is for us to bear the same relation to Him that the first sort of branches bear to the vine; that is to say, to abide in Christ is to renounce any independent life of our own, to give up trying to think our thoughts, or form our resolutions, or cultivate our feelings, and simply and constantly look to Christ to think His thoughts in us, to form His purposes in us, to feel His emotions and affections in us. It is to renounce all life independent of Christ, and constantly to look to Him for the inflow of His life into us, and the outworking of His life through us. When we do this, and in so far as we do this, our prayers will obtain that which we seek from God.

This must necessarily be so, for our desires will not be our own desires, but Christ's, and our prayers will not in reality be our own prayers, but Christ praying in us. Such prayers will always be in harmony with God's will, and the Father heareth Him always. When our prayers fail it is because they are indeed our prayers. We have conceived the desire and framed the petition of ourselves, instead of looking to Christ to pray through us.

To say that one should be abiding in Christ in all his prayers, looking to Christ to pray through Him rather than praying himself, is simply saying in another way that one should pray "in the Spirit." When we thus abide in Christ, our thoughts are not our own thoughts, but His, our joys are not our own joys, but His, our fruit is not our own fruit, but His; just as the buds, leaves, blossoms and fruit of the branch that abides in the vine are not the buds, leaves, blossoms and fruit of the branch, but of the vine itself whose life is flowing into the branch and manifests itself in these buds, leaves, blossoms and fruit.

To abide in Christ, one must of course already be in Christ through the acceptance of Christ as an atoning Savior from the guilt of sin, a risen Savior from the power of sin, and a Lord and Master over all his life. Being in Christ, all that we have to do to abide (or continue) in Christ is simply to renounce our self-life—utterly renouncing every thought, every purpose, every desire, every affection of our own, and just looking day by day and hour by hour for Jesus Christ to form His thoughts, His purposes, His affections, His desires in us. Abiding in Christ is really a very simple matter, though it is a wonderful life of privilege and of power.

2. "My Words Abide In You"

But there is another condition stated in this verse, though it is really involved in the first: "And My words abide in you."

If we are to obtain from God all that we ask from Him, Christ's words must abide or continue in us. We must study His words, fairly devour His words, let them sink into our thought and into our heart, keep them in our memory, obey them constantly in our life, let them shape and mold our daily life and our every act.

This is really the method of abiding in Christ. It is through His words that Jesus imparts Himself to us. The words He speaks unto us, they are spirit and they are life. (John 6:33) It is vain to expect power in prayer unless we meditate much upon the words of Christ, and let them sink deep and find a permanent abode in our hearts. There are many who wonder why they are so powerless in prayer, but the very simple explanation of it all is found in their neglect of the words of Christ. They have not hidden His words in their hearts; His words do not abide in them. It is not by seasons of mystical meditation and rapturous experiences that we learn to abide in Christ; it is by feeding upon His word, His written word as found in the Bible, and looking to the Holy Spirit to implant these words in our hearts and to make them a living thing in our hearts. If we thus let the words of Christ abide in us, they will stir us up in prayer. They will be the mold in which our prayers are shaped, and our prayers will be necessarily along the line of God's will, and will prevail with Him. Prevailing prayer is almost an impossibility where there is neglect of the study of the Word of God.

Mere intellectual study of the Word of God is not enough; there must be meditation upon it. The Word of God must be revolved over and over and over in the mind, with a constant looking to God by His Spirit to make that Word a living thing in the heart. The prayer that is born of meditation upon the Word of God is the prayer that soars upward most easily to God's listening ear.

George Muller, one of the mightiest men of prayer of the present generation, when the hour for prayer came, would begin by reading and meditating upon God's Word, until out of the study of the Word a prayer began to form itself in his heart. Thus God Himself was a real author of the prayer, and God answered the prayers which He Himself had inspired.

The Word of God is the instrument through which the Holy Spirit works, it is the sword of the Spirit in more senses than one; and the one who would know the work of the Holy Spirit in any direction must feed upon the Word. The one who would pray in the Spirit must meditate much upon the Word, that the Holy Spirit may have something through which He can work. The Holy Spirit works His prayers in us through the Word, and neglect of the Word makes praying in the Holy Spirit an impossibility. If we would feed the fire of our prayers with the fuel of God's Word, all our difficulties in prayer would disappear.

CHAPTER 8

Praying with Thanksgiving

There are two words often overlooked in the lesson about prayer which Paul gives us in Phil. 4:6,7:

> In nothing be anxious; but in everything by prayer and supplication with thanksgiving let your requests be made known unto God. And the peace of God, which passeth all understanding, shall guard your hearts and your thoughts in Christ Jesus. (RV)

The two important words often overlooked are, *"with thanksgiving."*

In approaching God to ask for new blessings, we should never forget to return thanks for blessings already granted. If any one of us would stop and think how many of the prayers which we have offered to God have been answered, and how seldom we have gone back to God to return thanks for the answers thus given, I am sure we would be overwhelmed with confusion. We should be just as definite in returning thanks as we are in prayer. We come to God with most specific petitions, but when we return thanks to Him, our thanksgiving is indefinite and general.

Doubtless one reason why so many of our prayers lack power is because we have neglected to return thanks for blessings already received. If any one were to constantly come to us asking help from us, and should never say "Thank you" for the help thus given, we would soon tire of helping one so ungrateful. Indeed, regard for the one we were helping would hold us back from encouraging such rank ingratitude. Doubtless our heavenly Father, out of a wise regard for our highest welfare, oftentimes refuses to answer petitions that we send up to Him in order that we may be brought to a sense of our ingratitude and taught to be thankful.

God is deeply grieved by the thanklessness and ingratitude of which so many of us are guilty. When Jesus healed the ten lepers and only one came back to give Him thanks, in wonderment and pain He exclaimed,

"Were not the ten cleansed? But where are the nine?" (Luke 17:17 RV)

How often must He look down upon us in sadness at our forgetfulness of His repeated blessings, and His frequent answer to our prayers.

Returning thanks for blessings already received increases our faith and enables us to approach God with new boldness and new assurance. Doubtless the reason so many have so little faith when they pray, is because they take so little time to meditate upon and thank God for blessings already received. As one meditates upon the answers to prayers already granted, faith waxes bolder and bolder, and we come to feel in the very depths of our souls that there is nothing too hard for the Lord. As we reflect upon the wondrous goodness of God toward us on the one hand, and upon the other hand upon the little thought and strength and time that we ever put into thanksgiving, we may well humble ourselves before God and confess our sin.

The mighty men of prayer in the Bible, and the mighty men of prayer throughout the ages of the church's history have been men who were much given to thanksgiving and praise. David was a mighty man of prayer, and how his Psalms abound with thanksgiving and praise. The apostles were mighty men of prayer; of them we read that "they were continually in the temple, praising and blessing God." Paul was a mighty man of prayer, and how often in his epistles he bursts out in definite thanksgiving to God for definite blessings and definite answers to prayers. Jesus is our model in prayer as in everything else. We find in the study of His life that His manner of returning thanks at the simplest meal was so noticeable that two of His disciples recognized Him by this after His resurrection.

Thanksgiving is one of the inevitable results of being filled with the Holy Spirit, and one who does not learn "in everything to give thanks" cannot continue to pray in the Spirit. If we would learn to pray with power we would do well to let these two words sink deep into our hearts: *"with thanksgiving."*

CHAPTER 9

Hindrances to Prayer

We have gone very carefully into the positive conditions of prevailing prayer; but there are some things which hinder prayer. These God has made very plain in His Word.

1. Asking Amiss

The first hindrance to prayer we will find in James 4: "Ye ask and receive not *because ye ask amiss, that ye may spend it in your pleasures.*"

A selfish purpose in prayer robs prayer of power. Very many prayers are selfish. These may be prayers for things for which it is perfectly proper to ask, for things which it is the will of God to give, but the motive of the prayer is entirely wrong, and so the prayer falls powerless to the ground. The true purpose in prayer is that God may be glorified in the answer. If we ask any petition merely that we may receive something to use in our pleasures or in our own gratification in one way or another, we "ask amiss" and need not expect to receive what we ask. This explains why many prayers remain unanswered.

For example, many a woman is praying for the conversion of her husband. That certainly is a most proper thing to ask; but many a woman's motive in asking for the conversion of her husband is entirely improper: it is selfish. She desires that her husband may be converted because it would be so much more pleasant for her to have a husband who sympathized with her; or it is so painful to think that her husband might die and be lost forever. For some such selfish reason as this she desires to have her husband converted. The prayer is purely selfish. Why should a woman desire the conversion of her husband? First of all and above all, that God may be glorified; because she cannot bear the thought that God the Father should be dishonored by her husband trampling underfoot the Son of God.

Many pray for a revival. That certainly is a prayer that is pleasing to God, it is along the line of His will; but many prayers for revivals are purely selfish. The churches desire revivals in order that the membership may be increased, in order that the church may have a position of more power and influence in the community, in order that the church treasury may be filled, in order that a good report may be made at the presbytery or conference or association. For such low purposes as these, churches and ministers oftentimes are praying for a revival, and oftentimes too God does not answer the prayer. Why should we pray for a revival? For the glory of God, because we cannot endure it that God should continue to be dishonored by the worldliness of the church, by the sins of unbelievers, by the proud unbelief of the day; because God's Word is being made void; in order that God may be glorified by the outpouring of His Spirit on the Church of Christ. For these reasons first of all and above all, we should pray for a revival.

Many a prayer for the Holy Spirit is a purely selfish prayer.

It certainly is God's will to give the Holy Spirit to them that ask Him— He has told us so plainly in His Word (Luke 11:13)—but many a prayer for the Holy Spirit is hindered by the selfishness of the motive that lies back of the prayer. Men and women pray for the Holy Spirit in order that they may be happy, or in order that they may be saved from the wretchedness of defeat in their lives, or in order that they may have power as Christian workers, or for some other purely selfish motive. Why should we pray for the Spirit? In order that God may no longer be dishonored by the low level of our Christian lives and by our ineffectiveness in service, in order that God may be glorified in the new beauty that comes into our lives and the new power that comes into our service.

2. Sin In the Way

The second hindrance to prayer we find in Is. 59:1,2.

Behold, the Lord's hand is not shortened, that it cannot save; neither His ear heavy, that it cannot hear. But *your iniquities have separated between you and your God, and your sins have hid his face from you, that he will not hear.* . . .

Sin hinders prayer. Many a man prays and prays and prays, and gets absolutely no answer to his prayer. Perhaps he is tempted to think that it is not the will of God to answer, or he may think that the days when God answered prayer, if He ever did, are over. So the Israelites seem to have thought. They thought that the Lord's hand was shortened, that it could not save, and that His ear had become heavy that it could no longer hear.

"Not so," said Isaiah, "God's ear is just as open to hear as ever, His hand just as mighty to save; but there is a hindrance. That hindrance is your own sins. Your iniquities have separated between you and your God, and your sins have hid His face from you that He will not hear."

It is so today. Many and many a man is crying to God in vain, simply because of sin in his life. It may be some sin in the past that has been unconfessed and unjudged, it may be some sin in the present that is cherished, very likely is not even looked upon as sin, but there the sin is, hidden away somewhere in the heart or in the life, and God "will not hear."

Any one who finds his prayers ineffective should not conclude that the thing which he asks of God is not according to His will, but should go alone with God with the Psalmist's prayer, "Search me, O God, and know my heart: try me, and know my thoughts: and see if there be any wicked way in me" (Ps. 139:23,24), and wait before Him until He puts His finger upon the thing that is displeasing in His sight. Then this sin should be confessed and put away.

I well remember a time in my life when I was praying for two definite things that it seemed that I must have, or God would be dishonored; but the answer did not come. I awoke in the middle of the night in great physical suffering and great distress of soul. I cried to God for these things, reasoned with Him as to how necessary it was that I get them, and get them at once; but no answer came. I asked God to show me if there was anything wrong in my own life. Something came to my mind that had often come to it before, something definite but which I was unwilling to confess as sin. I said to God,

"If this is wrong I will give it up"; but still no answer came. In my innermost heart, though I had never admitted it, I knew it was wrong.

At last I said:

"This is wrong. I have sinned. I will give it up."

I found peace. In a few moments I was sleeping like a child.

In the morning I woke well in body, and the money that was so much needed for the honor of God's name came.

Sin is an awful thing, and one of the most awful things about it is the way it hinders prayer, the way it severs the connection between us and the source of all grace and power and blessing. Any one who would have power in prayer must be merciless in dealing with his own sins. "If I regard iniquity in my heart, the Lord will not hear me." (Ps. 66:18) So long as we hold on to sin or have any controversy with God, we cannot expect Him to heed our prayers. If there is anything that is constantly coming up in your moments of close communion with God, that is the thing that hinders prayer: put it away.

3. Idols of the Heart

The third hindrance to prayer is found in Ez. 14:3:

Son of man, these men have taken their idols into their heart, and put the stumbling block of their iniquity before their face: should I be inquired of at all by them? (RV)

Idols in the heart cause God to refuse to listen to our prayers.

What is an idol? An idol is anything that takes the place of God, anything that is the supreme object of our affection. God alone has the right to the supreme place in our hearts. Everything and everyone else must be subordinate to Him.

Many a man makes an idol of his wife. Not that a man can love his wife any too much, but he can put her in the wrong place, he can put her before God; and when a man regards his wife's pleasure before God's pleasure, when he gives her the first place and God the second place, his wife is an idol, and God cannot hear his prayers.

Many a woman makes an idol of her children. Not that we can love our children too much. The more dearly we love Christ, the more dearly we love our children; but we can put our children in the wrong place, we can put them before God, and their interests before God's interests. When we do this, our children are our idols.

Many a man makes an idol of his reputation or his business. Reputation or business is put before God. God cannot hear the prayers of such a man.

One great question for us to decide, if we would have power in prayer is, "Is God absolutely first?" Is He before wife, before children, before reputation, before business, before our own lives? If not, prevailing prayer is impossible.

God often calls our attention to the fact that we have an idol, by not answering our prayers, and thus leading us to inquire as to why our prayers are not answered, and so we discover the idol, put it away, and God hears our prayers.

4. Lack of Care For the Poor

The fourth hindrance to prayer is found in Prov. 21:13, *"whoso stoppeth his ears at the cry of the poor, he also shall cry himself, but shall not be heard."*

There is perhaps no greater hindrance to prayer than stinginess, the lack of liberality toward the poor and toward God's work. It is the one who gives generously to others who receives generously from God. "Give, and it shall be given unto you; good measure, pressed down, shaken together, running over, shall they give into your bosom. For with what measure ye mete it shall be measured to you again." (Luke 6:38 RV) The generous man is the mighty man of prayer. The stingy man is the powerless man of prayer.

One of the most wonderful statements about prevailing prayer (already referred to) is 1 John 3:22, "Whatsoever we ask we receive of Him, because we keep His commandments, and do those things that are pleasing in His sight." It is made in direct connection with generosity toward the needy. In the context we are told that it is when we love, not in word or in tongue, but in deed and in truth, when we open our hearts toward the brother in need, it is then and only then we have confidence toward God in prayer.

Many a man and woman who is seeking to find the secret of their powerlessness in prayer need not seek far; it is nothing more nor less than downright stinginess. George Muller, to whom reference has already been made, was a mighty man of prayer because he was a mighty giver. What he received from God never stuck to his fingers; he immediately passed it on to others. He was constantly receiving because he was constantly giving. When one thinks of the selfishness of the professing church today, how the orthodox churches of this land do not average $1.00 per year per member for foreign missions, it is no wonder that the church has so little power in prayer. If we would get from God, we must give to others. Perhaps the most wonderful promise in the Bible in regard to God's supplying our need is Phil. 4:19, "And my God shall fulfill every need of yours according to His riches in glory in Christ Jesus." (RV) This glorious promise was made to the Philippian church, and made in immediate connection with their generosity.

5. Lack of Forgiveness

The fifth hindrance to prayer is found in Mark 11:25, "And when ye stand praying, *forgive,* if ye have ought against any; that your Father also which is in heaven may forgive you your trespasses."

An unforgiving spirit is one of the commonest hindrances to prayer. Prayer is answered on the basis that our sins are forgiven; and God cannot deal with us on the basis of forgiveness while we are harboring ill will against those who have wronged us. Any one who is nursing a grudge against another has fast closed the ear of God against his own petition. How many there are crying to God for the conversion of husband, children, friends; and wondering why it is that their prayer is not answered, when the whole secret is some grudge that they have in their hearts against someone who has injured them, or who they fancy has injured them. Many and many a mother and father are allowing their children to go down to eternity unsaved, for the miserable gratification of hating somebody.

6. Damaged Marriage Relationships

The sixth hindrance to prayer is found in 1 Peter 3:7, "Ye husbands, in like manner, dwell with your wives according to knowledge, giving honor unto the woman, as unto the weaker vessel as being also joint-heirs of the grace of life; to the end that your prayers be not hindered." (RV) Here we are plainly told that *a wrong relation between husband and wife is a hindrance to prayer.*

In many and many a case the prayers of husbands are hindered because of their failure of duty toward their wives. On the other hand, it is also doubtless true that the prayers of wives are hindered because of their failure in duty toward their husbands. If husbands and wives should seek diligently to find the cause of their unanswered prayers, they would often find it in their relations to one another.

Many a man who makes great pretensions to piety, and is very active in Christian work, shows but little consideration in his treatment of his wife, and is oftentimes unkind, if not brutal; then he wonders why it is that his prayers are not answered. The verse that we have just quoted explains the seeming mystery. On the other hand, many a woman who is very devoted to the church, and very faithful in attendance upon all services, treats her husband with the most unpardonable neglect, is cross and peevish toward him, wounds him by the sharpness of her speech, and by her ungovernable temper; then wonders why it is that she has no power in prayer.

There are other things in the relations of husbands and wives which cannot be spoken of publicly, but which doubtless are oftentimes a hindrance in approaching God in prayer. There is much of sin covered up under the holy name of marriage that is a cause of spiritual deadness, and of powerlessness in prayer. Any man or woman whose prayers seem to bring no answer should spread their whole married life out before God, and ask Him to put His finger upon anything in it that is displeasing in His sight.

7. Doubt

The seventh hindrance to prayer is found in James 1:5–7.

> But if any of you lacketh wisdom, let him ask of God, who giveth to all liberally and upbraideth not; and it shall be given him. But let him ask *in faith, nothing doubting:* for he that doubteth is like the surge of the sea driven by the wind and tossed. For let not that man think that he shall receive anything of the Lord. (RV)

Prayers are hindered by unbelief. God demands that we shall believe His Word absolutely. To question it is to make Him a liar. Many of us do that when we plead His promises, and is it any wonder that our prayers are not answered? How many prayers are hindered by our wretched unbelief! We go to God and ask Him for something that is positively promised in His Word, and then we do not more than half expect to get it. "Let not that man think that he shall receive anything of the Lord."

Chapter 10

When to Pray

If we would know the fullness of blessing that there is in the prayer life, it is important not only that we pray in the right way, but also that we pray at the right time. Christ's own example is full of suggestiveness as to the right time for prayer.

1. In the Morning

In the first chapter of Mark, the 35th verse, we read, "And *in the morning*, rising up *a great while before day*, He went out, and departed into a solitary place, and there prayed."

Jesus chose the early morning hour for prayer. Many of the mightiest men of God have followed the Lord's example in this. In the morning hour the mind is fresh and at its very best. It is free from distraction, and that absolute concentration upon God, which is essential to the most effective prayer, is most easily possible in the early morning hours. Furthermore, when the early hours are spent in prayer, the whole day is sanctified, and power is obtained for overcoming its temptations, and for performing its duties. More can be accomplished in prayer in the first hours of the day than at any other time during the day. Every child of God who would make the most out of his life for Christ, should set apart the first part of the day to meeting God in the study of His Word and in prayer. The first thing we do each day should be to go alone with God and face the duties, the temptations, and the service of that day, and get strength from God for all. We should get victory before the hour of trial, temptation or service comes. The secret place of prayer is the place to fight our battles and gain our victories.

2. All Night

In the sixth chapter of Luke in the twelfth verse, we get further light upon the right time to pray. We read, "And it came to pass in those days, that He went out into a mountain to pray, and continued *all night* in prayer to God."

Here we see Jesus praying in the night, spending the entire night in prayer. Of course we have no reason to suppose that this was the constant practice of our Lord, nor do we even know how common this practice was, but there were certainly times when the whole night was given up to prayer. Here too we do well to follow in the footsteps of the Master.

Of course there is a way of setting apart nights for prayer in which there is no profit; it is pure legalism. But the abuse of this practice is no reason for neglecting it altogether. One ought not to say, "I am going to spend a whole night in prayer," with the thought that there is any merit that will win God's favor in such an exercise; that is legalism. But we oftentimes do well to say, "I am going to set apart this night for meeting God, and obtaining His blessing and power; and if necessary, and if He so leads me, I will give the whole night to prayer." Oftentimes we will have prayed things through long before the night has passed, and we can retire and find more refreshing and invigorating sleep than if we had not spent the time in prayer. At other times God doubtless will keep us in communion with Himself away into the morning, and when He does this in His infinite grace, blessed indeed are these hours of night prayer!

Nights of prayer to God are followed by days of power with men. In the night hours the world is hushed in slumber, and we can easily be alone with God and have undisturbed communion with Him. If we set apart the whole night for prayer, there will be no hurry, there will be time for our own hearts to become quiet before God, there will be time for the whole mind to be brought under the guidance of the Holy Spirit, there will be plenty of time to pray things through. A night of prayer should be put entirely under God's control. We should lay down no rules as to how long we will pray, or as to what we shall pray about, but be ready to wait upon God for a short time or a long time as He may lead, and to be led out in one direction or another as He may see fit.

3. Before Crises

Jesus Christ prayed *before all the great crises in his earthly life.*

He prayed before choosing the twelve disciples; before the Sermon on the Mount; before starting out on an evangelistic tour; before His anointing with the Holy Spirit and His entrance upon His public ministry; before announcing to the twelve His approaching death; before the great consummation of His life at the cross. (Luke 6:12,13; Luke 9:18,21,22; Luke 3:21,22; Mark 1:35–38; Luke 22:39–46) He prepared for every important crisis by a protracted season of prayer. So ought we to do also. Whenever any crisis of life is seen to be approaching, we should prepare for it by a season of very definite prayer to God. We should take plenty of time for this prayer.

4. After Triumphs and Crises

Christ prayed not only before the great events and victories of His life, but He also prayed *after its great achievements and important crises.*

When He had fed the five thousand with the five loaves and two fishes, and the multitude desired to take Him and make Him king, having sent them away He went up into the mountain apart to pray, and spent hours there alone in prayer to God (Matt. 14:23; Jn. 6:15). So He went on from victory to victory.

It is more common for most of us to pray before the great events of life than it is to pray after them, but the latter is as important as the former. If we would pray after the great achievements of life, we might go on to still greater; as it is we are often either puffed up or exhausted by the things that we do in the name of the Lord, and so we advance no further. Many and many a man in answer to prayer has been endued with power and thus has wrought great things in the name of the Lord, and when these great things were accomplished, instead of going alone with God and humbling himself before Him, and giving Him all the glory for what was achieved, he has congratulated himself upon what has been accomplished, has become puffed up, and God has been obliged to lay him aside. The great things done were not followed by humiliation of self, and prayer to God, and so pride has come in and the mighty man has been shorn of his power.

5. When Life Is Very Busy

Jesus Christ gave a special time to prayer *when life was unusually busy.* He would withdraw at such a time from the multitudes that thronged about Him, and go into the wilderness and pray. For example, we read in Luke 5:15,16:

> But so much the more went abroad the report concerning Him: and great multitudes came together to hear, and to be healed of their infirmities. But He withdrew Himself in the deserts and prayed. (RV)

Some men are so busy that they find no time for prayer. Apparently the busier Christ's life was, the more He prayed. Sometimes He had no time to eat (Mark 3:20), sometimes He had no time for needed rest and sleep (Mark 6:31,33,46), but He always took time to pray; and the more the work crowded, the more He prayed.

Many a mighty man of God has learned this secret from Christ, and when the work has crowded more than usual they have set an unusual amount of time apart for prayer. Other men of God, once mighty, have lost their power because they did not learn this secret, and allowed increasing work to crowd out prayer.

Years ago it was this writer's privilege, with other theological students, to ask questions of one of the most useful Christian men of the day. The writer was led to ask, "Will you tell us something of your prayer life?"

The man was silent a moment, and then, turning his eyes earnestly upon me, replied:

"Well, I must admit that I have been so crowded with work of late that I have not given the time I should to prayer."

Is it any wonder that that man lost power, and the great work that he was doing was curtailed in a very marked degree? Let us never forget that the more the work presses on us, the more time must we spend in prayer.

6. Before Great Temptations

Jesus Christ prayed *before the great temptations of his life.*

As He drew nearer and nearer to the cross, and realized that upon it was to come the great final test of His life, Jesus went out into the garden to pray. He came "unto a place called Gethsemane, and saith unto the disciples, Sit ye here while I go and pray yonder." (Matt. 26:36) The victory of Calvary was won that night in the garden of Gethsemane. The calm majesty of His bearing in meeting the awful onslaughts of Pilate's Judgment Hall and of Calvary, was the outcome of the struggle, agony and victory of Gethsemane. While Jesus prayed, the disciples slept, so He stood fast while they fell ignominiously.

Many temptations come upon us unawares and unannounced, and all that we can do is to lift a cry to God for help then and there; but many of the temptations of life we can see approaching from the distance, and in such cases the victory should be won before the temptation really reaches us.

7. Without Ceasing, In All Seasons

In 1 Thess. 5:17 we read, "Pray *without ceasing,*" and in Eph. 6:18 RV, "praying *at all seasons.*"

Our whole life should be a life of prayer. We should walk in constant communion with God. There should be a constant upward looking of the soul to God. We should walk so habitually in His presence that even when we awake in the night it would be the most natural thing in the world for us to speak to Him in thanksgiving or in petition.

CHAPTER 11

The Need of a General Revival

If we are to pray aright in such a time as this, much of our prayer should be for a general revival. If there was ever a time in which there was need to cry unto God in the words of the Psalmist, "Wilt Thou not revive us again, that Thy people may rejoice in Thee?" (Ps. 85:6) It is this day in which we live. It is surely time for the Lord to work, for men have made void His law. (Ps. 119:126) The voice of the Lord given in the written Word is set at naught both by the world and the church. Such a time is not a time for discouragement—the man who believes in God and believes in the Bible can never be discouraged; but it is a time for Jehovah Himself to step in and word. The intelligent Christian, the wide-awake watchman on the walls of Zion, may well cry with the Psalmist of old, "It is time for Jehovah to work, for they have made void Thy law." (Ps. 119:126, Am. Revised Version)

The great need of the day is a general revival.

Let us consider first of all what a general revival is.

A revival is a time of quickening or impartation of life. As God alone can give life, a revival is a time when God visits His people and by the power of His Spirit imparts new life to them, and through them imparts life to sinners dead in trespasses and sins. We have religious excitements gotten up by the cunning methods and hypnotic influence of the mere professional evangelist; but these are not revivals and are not needed. They are the devil's imitations of a revival. *New life from God*—that is a revival. A general revival is a time when this new life from God is not confined to scattered localities, but is general throughout Christendom and the earth.

The reason why a general revival is needed is that spiritual dearth, and desolation, and death are general. It is not confined to any one country, though it may be more manifest in some countries than in others. It is found in foreign mission fields as well as in home fields. We have had local revivals. The life-giving Spirit of God has breathed upon this minister and that, this church and that, this community and that; but we need, we sorely need, a revival that shall be widespread and general.

Let us look for a few moments at the results of a revival. These results are apparent in ministers, in the church and in the unsaved.

1. The effect of revival on ministers.

The results of a revival in a minister are:

A. *The minister has a new love for souls.*

We ministers as a rule have no such love for souls as we ought to have, no such love for souls as Jesus had, no such love for souls as Paul had. But when God visits His people, the hearts of ministers are greatly burdened for the unsaved. They go out in great longing for the salvation of their fellow men. They forget their ambition to preach great sermons and for fame, and simply long to see men brought to Christ.

B. *When true revivals come, ministers get a new love for God's Word and a new faith in God's Word.*

They fling to the winds their doubts and criticisms of the Bible and of the creeds, and go to preaching the Bible and especially Christ crucified.

Revivals make ministers who are loose in their doctrines orthodox. A genuine wide sweeping revival would do more to turn things upside down and thus get them right side up than all the heresy trials ever instituted.

C. Revivals bring to ministers new liberty and power in preaching.

It is no week-long grind to prepare a sermon, and no nerve-consuming effort to preach it after it has been prepared. Preaching is a joy and a refreshment. There is power in it in times of revival.

2. The effect of revival on Christians.

The results of a revival on Christians generally are as marked as its results upon the ministry.

A. In times of revival Christians come out from the world and live separated lives.

Christians who have been dallying with the world, who have been playing cards and dancing and going to the theater and indulging in similar follies, give them up. These things are found to be incompatible with increasing life and light.

B. In times of revival Christians get a new spirit of prayer.

Prayer meetings are no longer a duty, but become the necessity of a hungry, importunate heart. Private prayer is followed with new zest. The voice of earnest prayer to God is heard day and night. People no longer ask, "Does God answer prayer?" They know He does, and besiege the throne of grace day and night.

C. In times of revival Christians go to work for lost souls.

They do not go to meeting simply to enjoy themselves and get blessed. They go to meeting to watch for souls and to bring them to Christ. They talk to men on the street and in the stores and in their homes. The cross of Christ, salvation, heaven, and hell become the subjects of constant conversation. Politics and the weather and new bonnets and the latest novels are forgotten.

D. *In times of revival Christians have new joy in Christ.*

Life is joy, and new life is new joy. Revival days are glad days, days of heaven on earth.

E. *In times of revival Christians get a new love for the Word of God.*

They want to study it day and night. Revivals are bad for saloons and theaters, but they are good for bookstores and Bible agencies.

3. The effect of revival on non-Christians.

But revivals also have a decided influence on the unsaved world.

A *First of all, they bring deep conviction of sin.*

Jesus said that when the Spirit was come He would convince the world of sin. (Jn. 16:7, 8) Now we have seen that a revival is a coming of the Holy Spirit, and therefore there must be a new conviction of sin, and there always is. If you see something men call a revival, and there is no conviction of sin, you may know at once that it is bogus. It is a sure mark.

B. *Revivals bring also conversion and regeneration.*

When God refreshes His people, He always converts sinners also. The first result of Pentecost was new life and power to the one hundred and twenty disciples in the upper room; the second result was three thousand conversions in a single day. It is always so. I am constantly reading of revivals here and there, where Christians were greatly helped, but there were no conversions. I have my doubts about that kind. If Christians are truly refreshed, they will get after the unsaved by prayer and testimony and persuasion, and there will be conversions.

Why A General Revival Is Needed

We see what a general revival is, and what it does; let us now face the question why it is needed at the present time.

I think that the mere description of what it is and what it does shows that it is needed, sorely needed, but let us look at some specific conditions that exist today that show the need of it. In showing these conditions one is likely to be called a pessimist. If facing the facts is to be called a pessimist,

I am willing to be called a pessimist. If in order to be an optimist, one must shut his eyes and call black white, and error truth, and sin righteousness, and death life, I don't want to be called an optimist. But I am an optimist all the same. Pointing out the real condition will lead to a better condition.

1. Renewed faith in the ministry.

Look first at the ministry.

A. Many of us who are professedly orthodox ministers are practically infidels.

That is plain speech, but it is also indisputable fact. There is no essential difference between the teachings of Tom Paine and Bob Ingersoll and the teachings of some of our theological professors. The latter are not so blunt and honest about it; they phrase it in more elegant and studied sentences; but it means the same. Much of the so-called new learning and higher criticism is simply Tom Paine infidelity sugar-coated. Prof. Howard Osgood, who is a real scholar and not a mere echo of German infidelity, once read a statement of some positions, and asked if they did not fairly represent the scholarly criticism of today. When it was agreed that they did, he startled his audience by saying:

"I am reading from Tom Paine's *Age of Reason.*"

There is little new in the higher criticism. Our future ministers oftentimes are being educated under infidel professors, and being immature boys when they enter the college or seminary, they naturally come out infidels in many cases, and then go forth to poison the church.

B. Even when our ministers are orthodox—as thank God so very many are!—they are oftentimes not men of prayer.

How many modern ministers know what it is to wrestle in prayer, to spend a good share of a night in prayer? I do not know how many, but I do know that many *do not.*

C. Many of us who are ministers have no love for souls.

How many preach because they *must* preach, because they feel that men everywhere are perishing, and by preaching they hope to save some?

And how many follow up their preaching as Paul did, by beseeching men everywhere to be reconciled to God?

Perhaps enough has been said about us ministers; but it is evident that a revival is needed for our sake or some of us will have to stand before God overwhelmed with confusion in an awful day of reckoning that is surely coming.

2. Refreshed doctrine and spirituality in the church.

Look now at the church.

A. Look at the doctrinal state of the church.

It is bad enough. Many do not believe in the whole Bible. The book of Genesis is a myth, Jonah is an allegory, and even the miracles of the Son of God are questioned. The doctrine of prayer is old fashioned, and the work of the Holy Spirit is sneered at. Conversion is unnecessary, and hell is no longer believed in. Then look at the fads and errors that have sprung up out of this loss of faith: Christian Science, Unitarianism, spiritualism, Universalism, Babism, metaphysical healing, etc., etc., a perfect pandemonium of doctrines of devils.

B. Look at the spiritual state of the church.

Worldliness is rampant among church members. Many church members are just as eager as any in the rush to get rich. They use the methods of the world in the accumulation of wealth, and they hold just as fast to it as any when they have gotten it.

Prayerlessness abounds among church members on every hand. someone has said that Christians on the average do not spend more than five minutes a day in prayer.

Neglect of the Word of God goes hand in hand with neglect of prayer to God. Very many Christians spend twice as much time every day wallowing through the mire of the daily papers, as they do bathing in the cleansing laver [ritual wash basin] of God's Holy Word. How many Christians average an hour a day spent in Bible study?

Along with neglect of prayer and neglect of the Word of God goes a lack of generosity. The churches are rapidly increasing in wealth, but the treasuries of the missionary societies are empty. Christians do not average a dollar a year for foreign missions. It is simply appalling.

Then there is the increasing disregard for the Lord's Day. It is fast becoming a day of worldly pleasure, instead of a day of holy service. The Sunday newspaper with its inane twaddle and filthy scandal takes the place of the Bible; and visiting and golf and bicycle, the place of the Sunday school and church service.

Christians mingle with the world in all forms of questionable amusements. The young man or young woman who does not believe in dancing with its rank immodesties, the card table with its drift toward gambling, and the theater with its ever-increasing appeal to lewdness, is counted an old fogy.

Then how small a proportion of our membership has really entered into fellowship with Jesus Christ in His burden for souls! Enough has been said of the spiritual state of the church.

3. Worsening moral condition in the world.

Now look at the state of the world.

A. Note how few conversions there are.

The Methodist church, which has led the way in aggressive work, has actually lost more members than it has gained the last year. Here and there a church has a large number of accessions upon confession of faith, but these churches are rare exceptions; and where there are such accessions, in how few cases are the conversions deep, thorough and satisfactory.

B. There is lack of conviction of sin.

Seldom are men overwhelmed with a sense of their awful guilt in trampling under foot the Son of God. Sin is regarded as a "misfortune" or as "infirmity," or even as "good in the making"; seldom as enormous wrong against a holy God.

C. Unbelief is rampant.

Many regard it as a mark of intellectual superiority to reject the Bible, and even faith in God and immortality. It is about the only mark of intellectual superiority many possess, and perhaps that is the reason they cling to it so tenaciously.

D. *Hand in hand with this widespread infidelity goes gross immorality, as has always been the case.*

Infidelity and immorality are Siamese twins. They always exist and always grow and always fatten together. This prevailing immorality is found everywhere.

Look at the legalized adultery that we call divorce. Men marry one wife after another, and are still admitted into good society; and women do likewise. There are thousands of supposedly respectable men in America living with other men's wives, and thousands of supposedly respectable women living with other women's husbands.

This immorality is found in the theater. The theater at its best is bad enough, but now "Sapphos," and the "Degenerates," and all the unspeakable vile accessories of the stage rule the day, and the women who debauch themselves by appearing in such plays are defended in the newspapers and welcomed by supposedly respectable people.

Much of our literature is rotten, but decent people will read books as bad as *Trilby* because it is the rage. Art is oftentimes a mere covering for shameless indecency. Women are induced to cast modesty to the winds that the artist may perfect his art and defile his morals.

Greed for money has become a mania with rich and poor. The multimillionaire will often sell his soul and trample the rights of his fellow men underfoot in the mad hope of becoming a billionaire, and the laboring man will often commit murder to increase the power of the union and keep up wages. Wars are waged and men shot down like dogs to improve commerce, and to gain political prestige for unprincipled politicians who parade as statesmen.

The licentiousness of the day lifts its serpent head everywhere. You see it in the newspapers, you see it on the billboards, you see it on the advertisements of cigars, shoes, bicycles, patent medicines, corsets, and everything else. You see it on the streets at night. You see it just outside the church door. You find it not only in the awful cesspools set apart for it in the great cities, but it is crowding further and further up our business streets and into the residence portions of our cities. Alas! now and then you find it, if you look sharp, in supposedly respectable homes; indeed it will be borne to your ears by the confessions of brokenhearted men and women. The moral condition of the world in our day is disgusting, sickening, appalling.

We need a revival: deep, widespread, general, in the power of the Holy Ghost. It is either a general revival or the dissolution of the church, of the home, of the state. A revival, new life from God, is the cure, and the only cure. That will stem the awful tide of immorality and unbelief. Mere argument will not do it; but a sign from heaven, a new outpouring of the Spirit of God. It was not discussion but the breath of God that relegated Tom Paine, Voltaire, Volney, and other of the old infidels to the limbo of forgetfulness; and we need a new breath from God to send the Wellhausens and the Kuenens and the Grafs and the parrots they have trained to occupy chairs and pulpits in England and America to keep them company. I believe that breath from God is coming.

The great need of today is a general revival. The need is clear. It admits of no honest difference of opinion. What then shall we do? Pray. Take up the Psalmist's prayer, "Revive us again, that Thy people may rejoice in Thee." Take up Ezekiel's prayer: "Come from the four winds, O breath (breath of God), and breathe upon these slain that they may live." Hark, I hear a noise! Behold a shaking! I can almost feel the breeze upon my cheek. I can almost see the great living army rising to their feet. Shall we not pray and pray and pray and pray, till the Spirit comes, and God revives His people?

CHAPTER 12

The Place of Prayer Before and During Revivals

No treatment of the subject "how to pray" would be at all complete if it did not consider the place of prayer in revivals.

The first great revival of Christian history had its origin on the human side in a ten-days' prayer meeting. We read of that handful of disciples, "These all with one accord continued steadfastly in prayer." (Acts 1:14 RV) The result of that prayer meeting we read of in the second chapter of the Acts of the Apostles, "They were all filled with the Holy Ghost, and began to speak with other tongues, as the Spirit gave them utterance." (v .4) Further on in the chapter we read that "there were added unto them in that day about three thousand souls." (v. 41 RV) This revival proved genuine and permanent. The converts "continued steadfastly in the apostles' teaching and fellowship, in the breaking of bread and the prayers." (v. 42 RV) "And the Lord added to them day by day those that were being saved." (v. 47 RV)

Every true revival from that day to this has had its earthly origin in prayer. The great revival under Jonathan Edwards in the 18th century began with his famous call to prayer. The marvelous work of grace among the Indians under

75

Brainerd had its origin in the days and nights that Brainerd spent before God in prayer for an enduement of power from on high for this work.

A most remarkable and widespread display of God's reviving power was that which broke out at Rochester, New York, in 1830, under the labors of Charles G. Finney. It not only spread throughout the state, but ultimately to Great Britain as well. Mr. Finney himself attributed the power of this work to the spirit of prayer that prevailed. He describes it in his autobiography in the following words.

> When I was on my way to Rochester, as we passed through a village, some thirty miles east of Rochester, a brother minister whom I knew, seeing me on the canal-boat, jumped aboard to have a little conversation with me, intending to ride but a little way and return. He, however, became interested in conversation, and upon finding where I was going, he made up his mind to keep on and go with me to Rochester. We had been there but a few days when this minister became so convinced that he could not help weeping aloud at one time as we passed along the street. The Lord gave him a powerful spirit of prayer, and his heart was broken. As he and I prayed together, I was struck with his faith in regard to what the Lord was going to do there. I recollect he would say, "Lord, I do not know how it is; but I seem to know that Thou art going to do a great work in this city." The spirit of prayer was poured out powerfully, so much so that some persons stayed away from the public services to pray, being unable to restrain their feelings under preaching.

> And here I must introduce the name of a man whom I shall have occasion to mention frequently, Mr. Abel Clary. He was the son of a very excellent man, and an elder of the church where I was converted. He was converted in the same revival in which I was. He had been licensed to preach; but his spirit of prayer was such, he was so burdened with the souls of men, that he was not able to preach much, his whole time and strength being given to prayer. The burden of his soul would frequently be so great that he was unable to stand, and he would writhe and groan in agony. I was well acquainted with him, and knew something of the wonderful spirit of prayer that was upon him. He was a very silent man, as almost all are who have that powerful spirit of prayer.

> The first I knew of his being in Rochester, a gentleman who lived about a mile west of the city, called on me one day and asked me if I knew a Mr. Abel Clary, a minister. I told him that I knew him well. "Well," he

said, "he is at my house, and has been there for some time, and I don't know what to think of him." I said, "I have not seen him at any of our meetings." "No," he replied, "he cannot go to meeting, he says. He prays nearly all the time, day and night, and in such agony of mind that I do not know what to make of it. Sometimes he cannot even stand on his knees, but will lie prostrate on the floor, and groan and pray in a manner that quite astonishes me." I said to the brother, "I understand it: please keep still. It will all come out right; he will surely prevail."

I knew at the time a considerable number of men who were exercised in the same way. A Deacon P—, of Camden, Oneida county; a Deacon T—, of Rodman, Jefferson county; a Deacon B—, of Adams, in the same county; this Mr. Clary and many others among the men, and a large number of women partook of the same spirit, and spent a great part of their time in prayer. Father Nash, as we called him, who in several of my fields of labor came to me and aided me, was another of those men that had such a powerful spirit of prevailing prayer. This Mr. Clary continued in Rochester as long as I did, and did not leave it until after I had left. He never, that I could learn, appeared in public [after I left], but gave himself wholly to prayer.

I think it was the second Sabbath that I was at Auburn at this time, I observed in the congregation the solemn face of Mr. Clary. He looked as if he was borne down with an agony of prayer. Being well acquainted with him, and knowing the great gift of God that was upon him, the spirit of prayer, I was very glad to see him there. He sat in the pew with his brother, the doctor, who was also a professor of religion, but who had nothing by experience, I should think, of his brother Abel's great power with God.

At intermission, as soon as I came down from the pulpit, Mr. Clary, with his brother, met me at the pulpit stairs, and the doctor invited me to go home with him and spend the intermission and get some refreshments. I did so.

After arriving at his house we were soon summoned to the dinner table. We gathered about the table, and Dr. Clary turned to his brother and said, "Brother Abel, will you ask the blessing?" Brother Abel bowed his head and began, audibly, to ask a blessing. He had uttered but a sentence or two when he broke instantly down, moved suddenly back from the table, and fled to his chamber. The doctor supposed he had been taken suddenly ill, and rose up and followed him. In a few moments he came down and said, "Mr. Finney, brother Abel wants to see you." Said I, "What ails him?" Said he, "I do not know, but he says you know. He appears in great distress, but I think it is the state of his mind." I understood it in a moment, and went to his room. He lay groaning upon the bed, the Spirit making intercession for him, and in him, with groanings that could not be uttered. I had barely entered the room, when he made out to say, "Pray, brother Finney." I knelt down and helped him in prayer, by leading his soul out for the conversion of sinners. I continued to pray until his distress passed away, and then I returned to the dinner table.

I understood that this was the voice of God. I saw the spirit of prayer was upon him, and I felt his influence upon myself, and took it for granted that the work would move on powerfully. It did so. The pastor told me afterward that he found that in the six weeks that I was there, five hundred souls had been converted.

Mr. Finney in his lectures on revivals tells of other remarkable awakenings in answer to the prayers of God's people. He says in one place,

A clergyman in W——n told me of a revival among his people, which commenced with a zealous and devoted woman in the church. She became anxious about sinners, and went to praying for them; she prayed, and her distress increased; and she finally came to her minister, and talked with him, and asked him to appoint an anxious meeting, for she felt that one was needed. The minister put her off, for he felt nothing of it. The next week she came again, and besought him to appoint an anxious meeting, she knew there would be somebody to come, for she felt as if God was going to pour out His Spirit. He put her off again. And finally she said to him, "If you do not appoint an anxious meeting I shall die, for there is certainly going to be a revival." The next Sabbath he appointed a meeting, and said that if there were any who wished to converse with him about the salvation of their souls, he would meet them on such an evening. He did not know of one, but when he went to the place, to his astonishment he found a large number of anxious inquirers.

In still another place he says,

The first ray of light that broke in upon the midnight which rested on the churches in Oneida county, in the fall of 1825, was from a woman in feeble health, who, I believe had never been in a powerful revival. Her soul was exercised about sinners. She was in agony for the land. She did not know what ailed her, but she kept praying more and more, till it seemed as if her agony would destroy her body. At length she became full of joy and exclaimed, "God has come! God has come! There is no mistake about it, the work is begun, and is going over all the region!" And sure enough, the work began, and her family were almost all converted, and the work spread all over that part of the country.

The great revival of 1857 in the United States began in prayer and was carried on by prayer more than by anything else. Dr. Cuyler, in an article in a religious newspaper some years ago said,

Most revivals have humble beginnings, and the fire starts in a few warm hearts. Never despise the day of small things. During all my own long ministry, nearly every work of grace had a similar beginning. One commenced in a meeting gathered at a few hours' notice in a private house. Another commenced in a group gathered for Bible study by Mr. Moody in our mission chapel. Still another—the most powerful of all—was kindled on a bitter January evening at a meeting of young Christians under my roof. Dr. Spencer, in his *Pastor's Sketches,* (the most suggestive book of its kind I have ever read), tells us that a remarkable revival in his church sprang from the fervent prayers of a godly old man who was confined to his room by lameness. That profound Christian, Dr. Thomas H. Skinner, of the Union Theological Seminary, once gave me an account of a remarkable coming together of three earnest men in his study when he was the pastor of the Arch Street Church in Philadelphia. They literally wrestled in prayer. They made a clean breast in confession of sin, and humbled themselves before God. One and another church officer came in and joined them. The heaven-kindled flame soon spread through the whole congregation in one of the most powerful revivals ever known in that city.

In the early part of the seventeenth century there was a great religious awakening in Ulster, Ireland. The lands of the rebel chiefs, which had been forfeited to the British crown, were settled up by a class of colonists who for the most part were governed by a spirit of wild adventure. Real piety was rare. Seven ministers, five from Scotland and two from England, settled in that country, the earliest arrivals being in 1613. Of one of these ministers named Blair, it is recorded by a contemporary, "He spent many days and nights in prayer, alone and with others, and was vouchsafed great intimacy with God." Mr. James Glendenning, a man of very meager natural gifts, was a man similarly minded as regards prayer. The work began under this man Glendenning. The historian of the time says,

> He was a man who never would have been chosen by a wise assembly of ministers nor sent to begin a reformation in this land. Yet this was the Lord's choice to begin with him the admirable work of God which I mention on purpose that all may see how the glory is only the Lord's in making a holy nation in this profane land, and that it was "not by might, nor by power, nor by man's wisdom, but by My Spirit, saith the Lord." In his preaching at Oldstone, multitudes of hearers felt in great anxiety and terror of conscience. They looked on themselves as altogether lost and damned, and cried out, "Men and brethren, what shall we do to be saved?" They were stricken into a swoon by the power of His Word. A dozen in one day were carried out of doors as dead. These were not women, but some of the boldest spirits of the neighborhood; "some who had formerly feared not with their swords to put a whole market town into a fray." Concerning one of them, then a mighty strong man, now a mighty Christian, say, that his end in coming into church was to consult with his companions how to work some mischief.

This work spread throughout the whole country. By the year 1626 a monthly concert of prayer was held in Antrim. The work spread beyond the bounds of Down and Antrim to the churches of the neighboring counties. So great became the religious interest that Christians would come thirty or forty miles to the communions, and continue from the time they came until they returned without wearying or making use of sleep. Many of them neither ate nor drank, and yet some of them professed that they "went away most fresh and vigorous, their souls so filled with the sense of God."

This revival changed the whole character of northern Ireland.

Another great awakening in Ireland in 1859 had a somewhat similar origin. By many who did not know, it was thought that this marvelous work came without warning and preparation, but Rev. William Gibson, the moderator of the General Assembly of the Presbyterian Church in Ireland in 1860, in his very interesting and valuable history of the work, tells how there had been preparation for two years. There had been constant discussion in the General Assembly of the low estate of religion, and of the need of a revival. There had been special sessions for prayer. Finally four young men, who became leaders in the origin of the great work, began to meet together in an old schoolhouse in the neighborhood of Kells. About the spring of 1858 a work of power began to manifest itself. It spread from town to town, and from county to county. The congregations became too large for the buildings, and the meetings were held in the open air, often-times attended by many thousands of people. Many hundreds of persons were frequently convicted of sin in a single meeting. In some places the criminal courts and jails were closed for lack of occupation. There were manifestations of the Holy Spirit's power of a most remarkable character, clearly proving that the Holy Spirit is as ready to work today as in apostolic days, when ministers and Christians really believe in Him and begin to pre-pare the way by prayer.

Mr. Moody's wonderful work in England and Scotland and Ireland that afterwards spread to America had its origin, on the manward side, in prayer. Mr. Moody made little impression until men and women began to cry to God. Indeed, his going to England at all was in answer to the impor-tunate cries to God of a bedridden saint. While the spirit of prayer contin-ued the revival abode in strength, but in the course of time less and less was made of prayer and the work fell off very perceptibly in power. Doubtless one of the great secrets of the unsatisfactoriness and superficiality and un-reality of many of our modern so-called revivals, is that more dependence is put upon man's machinery than upon God's power, sought and obtained by earnest, persistent, believing prayer. We live in a day characterized by the multiplication of man's machinery and the diminution of God's power. The great cry of our day is work, work, work; new organizations, new methods, new machinery; the great *need* of our day is *prayer*. It was a masterstroke of the devil when he got the church so generally to lay aside this mighty weapon of prayer. The devil is perfectly willing that the church should multiply its organizations, and deftly contrive machinery for the conquest of the world for Christ if it will only give up praying. He laughs as he looks at the church today and says to himself:

You can have your Sunday schools and your Young People's Societies, your Young Men's Christian Associations and your Women's Christian Temperance Unions, your Institutional Churches and your Industrial Schools, and your Boy's Brigades, your grand choirs and your fine or-gans, your brilliant preachers and your revival efforts too,—if you don't bring the power of Almighty God into them by earnest, persistent, believing, mighty prayer.

Prayer could work as marvelous results today as it ever could, if the church would only betake itself to it.

There seem to be increasing signs that the church is awakening to this fact. Here and there God is laying upon individual ministers and churches a burden of prayer that they have never known before. Less dependence is being put upon machinery and more dependence upon God. Ministers are crying to God day and night for power. Churches and portions of churches are meeting together in the early morning hours and the late night hours crying to God for the latter rain. There is every indication of the coming of a mighty and widespread revival. There is every reason why, if a revival should come in any country at this time, it should be more widespread in its extent than any revival of history. There is the closest and swiftest communication by travel, by letter, and by cable between all parts of the world. A true fire of God kindled in America would soon spread to the uttermost parts of the earth. The only thing needed to bring this fire is prayer.

It is not necessary that the whole church get to praying to begin with. Great revivals always begin first in the hearts of a few men and women whom God arouses by His Spirit to believe in Him as a living God, as a God who answers prayer, and upon whose heart He lays a burden from which no rest can be found except in importunate crying unto God.

May God use this book to arouse many others to pray that the greatly needed revival may come, and come speedily.

Let us pray!

How To Study The Bible

First Published 1896

Preface

This book has been written for two reasons: first, because it seemed to be needed; second, to save the writer time and labor. Letters are constantly coming in from all quarters asking how to study the Bible. It is impossible to refuse to answer a question so important as that, but it takes much time to answer it at all as it should be answered. This book is written as an answer to those who have asked the question, and to those who may wish to ask it.

Nothing is more important for our own mental, moral and spiritual development, or for our increase in usefulness, than Bible study. But not all Bible study is equally profitable. Some Bible study is absolutely profitless. "How to study the Bible so as to get the largest profit from it," is a question of immeasurable importance. The answer to the question, found in this book, has been for the most part given in addresses by this author, at the Chicago Bible Institute, before the summer gatherings of college students, at ministerial conferences and Y.M.C.A. conventions. Many, especially ministers, who have heard these addresses, have asked that they might be put in a permanent shape. I have promised for two years to comply with this request, but have never found time to do so until now.

—R. A. Torrey

PART I

The Methods of the Most Profitable Bible Study

CHAPTER 1

Introductory Chapter to Methods of Bible Study

We shall consider the most profitable *methods* of Bible study before we consider the fundamental *conditions* of profitable Bible study. Many readers of this book will probably be frightened, at first, at the seeming elaborateness and difficulty of some of the methods of study suggested. But they are not as difficult as they appear. Their practicability and fruitfulness have been tested in the classroom, and that not with classes made up altogether of college graduates, but largely composed of persons of very moderate education; in some cases of almost no education. They do require time and hard work. It must be remembered, however, that the Bible contains gold, and almost anyone is willing to dig for gold, especially if it is certain that he will find it. It is certain that one will find gold in the Bible, if he digs. As one uses the methods here recommended, he will find his ability to do the work rapidly increasing by exercise, until he can soon do more in fifteen minutes than at the outset he could do in an hour.

The first method of study suggested will be found to be an exceptionally good mental training. When one has pursued this method of study for

91

a time, his powers of observation will have been so quickened, that he will see at a glance what, at first, he only saw upon much study and reflection. This method of study will also train the logical powers, cultivating habits of order, system, and classification in one's intellectual processes. The power of clear, concise and strong expression will also be developed. No other book affords the opportunity for intellectual development by its study, as is to be found in the Bible. No other book, and no other subject, will so abundantly repay close and deep study. The Bible is much read, but comparatively little studied. It will probably be noticed by some that the first method of study suggested is practically the method now pursued in the study of nature; first, careful analysis and ascertainment of facts; second, classification of facts. But the facts of revelation far transcend those of nature in sublimity, suggestiveness, helpfulness, and practical utility. They are also far more accessible. We cannot all be profound students of nature; we can all be profound students of Scripture. Many an otherwise illiterate person has a marvelous grasp of Bible truth. It was acquired by study. There are persons who have studied little else, who have studied the Scriptures, by the hour, daily, and their consequent wisdom is the astonishment and sometimes dismay of scholars and theologians.

CHAPTER 2

The Study of Individual Books

The first method of Bible study that we shall consider is the *study of the Bible by individual books*. This method of study is the most thorough, the most difficult, and the one that yields the largest and most permanent results. We take it up first, because in the author's opinion, it should occupy the greater portion of our time.

I. Select A Book To Study

The first work to do is to select the book to study. This is a very important matter. If one makes an unfortunate selection he may become discouraged and give up a method of study that might have been most fruitful.

A few points will be helpful to the beginner:

1. For your first book study, choose a short book.

The choice of a long book to begin with will lead to discouragement in any one but a person of rare perseverance. It will be so long before the final results, which far more than pay for all the labor expended, are reached, that the ordinary student will give it up.

2. Choose a comparatively easy book.

Some books of the Bible present grave difficulties not to be found in other books. One will wish to meet and overcome these later, but it is not the work for a beginner to set for himself. When his powers have become trained by reason of use, then he can do this successfully and satisfactorily, but, if he attempts it, as so many rashly do, at the outset, he will soon find himself floundering. The First Epistle of Peter is an exceedingly precious book, but a few of the most difficult passages in the Bible are in it. If it were not for these difficult passages, it would be a good book to recommend to the beginner, but in view of these difficulties it is not wise to undertake to make it a subject of exhaustive study until later.

3. Choose a book that is rich enough in its teaching to illustrate the advantages of this method of study, and thus give a keen appetite for further studies of the same kind.

When one has gone through one reasonably large and full book by the method of study about to be described, he will have an eagerness for it that will make it sure that he will somehow find time for further studies of the same sort.

A book that meets all the conditions stated is the First Epistle of Paul to the Thessalonians. It is quite short, it has no great difficulties of interpretation, meaning or doctrine, and it is exceedingly rich in its teaching. It has the further advantage of being the first in point of time of the Pauline Epistles. The First Epistle of John is not in most respects a difficult book, and it is one of the richest books in the Bible.

II. Master the Book's General Contents

The second work to do is to master the general contents of the book. The method of doing this is very simple. It consists in merely reading the book through without stopping, and then reading it through again, and then again, say a dozen times in all, at a single sitting. To one who has never tried it, it does not seem as if that would amount to much, but any thoughtful man who has ever tried it will tell you quite differently. It is simply wonderful how a book takes on new meaning and beauty upon this sort of an acquaintance. It begins to open up. New relations between different parts of the book begin to disclose themselves. Fascinating lines of thought running through the book appear. The book is grasped as a whole, and the relation of the various parts to one another apprehended, and a foundation laid for an intelligent study of those parts in detail.

Rev. James M. Gray of Boston, a great lover of the Bible and prominent teacher of it, says that for many years of his ministry he had "an inadequate and unsatisfactory knowledge of the English Bible." The first practical idea which he received in the study of the English Bible was from a layman. The brother possessed an unusual serenity and joy in his Christian experience, which he attributed to his reading of the Epistle to the Ephesians.

Mr. Gray asked him how he had read it, and he said he had taken a pocket copy of the Epistle into the woods one Sunday afternoon, and read it through at a single sitting, repeating the process as many as a dozen times before stopping, and when he arose, he had gotten possession of the Epistle, or rather its wondrous truths had gotten possession of him. This was the secret, simple as it was, for which Mr. Gray had been waiting and praying. From this time on, Mr. Gray studied his Bible through in this way, and it became to him a new book.

III. Prepare an Introduction

The third work is to prepare an introduction to the book. Write down at the top of separate sheets of paper or cards the following questions: 1. Who wrote this book? 2. To whom did he write? 3. Where did he write it? 4. When did he write it? 5. What was the occasion of his writing? 6. What was the purpose for which he wrote? 7. What were the circumstances of the author when he wrote? 8. What were the circumstances of those to whom he wrote? 9. What glimpses does the book give into the life and character of the author? 10. What are the leading ideas of the book? 11. What is the central truth of the book? 12. What are the characteristics of the book?

Having prepared your sheets of paper with these questions at the head, lay them side by side on your study table before you, and go through the book slowly, and, as you come to an answer to any one of these questions, write it down on the appropriate sheet of paper. It may be necessary to go through the book several times to do the work thoroughly and satisfactorily, but you will be amply repaid. When you have finished your own work in this line, and not until then, it will be well, if possible, to compare your results with those reached by others. A book that will serve as a good illustration of this introductory work is *The New Testament and Its Writers,* by Rev. J. A. McClymont.

The introduction one prepares for himself will be worth many times more to him than any that he can procure from others. The work itself is a rare education of the faculties of perception, comparison and reasoning.

The answers to our questions will sometimes be found in some related book. For example, if we are studying one of the Pauline Epistles, the answer to our questions may be found in the Acts of the Apostles, or in the Epistle written to the place from which the one studied, was written. Of course, all the questions given will not apply to every book in the Bible.

If one is not willing to give the time and labor necessary, this introductory work can be omitted, but only at a great sacrifice. Single passages in an epistle can never be correctly understood unless we know to whom they were written. Much false interpretation of the Bible arises from taking some direction manifestly intended for local application to be of universal authority. So, also, oftentimes false interpretation arises from applying to the unbeliever what was intended for the saint.

Noting the occasion of writing will clear up the meaning of a passage that would be otherwise obscure. Bearing in mind the circumstances of the author when he wrote will frequently give new force to his words. When we remember that the jubilant epistle to the Philippians, with its oft-repeated "rejoice in the Lord" and its:

> . . . in nothing be anxious; but in everything by prayer and supplication with thanksgiving let your requests be made known unto God. And the peace of God, which passeth all understanding, shall guard your hearts and your thoughts in Christ Jesus . . .

was written by a prisoner awaiting possible sentence of death, how much more meaningful it becomes. Bearing in mind the main purpose for which a book was written, will help to interpret its incidental exhortations in their proper relations. In fact, the answers to all the questions will be valuable in all the work that follows, as well as valuable in themselves.

IV. Divide the Book Into Sections

The fourth work is to divide the book into its proper sections. This work is not indispensable, but still it is valuable. Go through the book and notice the principal divisions in the thought, and mark these. Then go through these divisions and find if there are any natural subdivisions and mark these. In this work of dividing the epistle, the Revised Version, which is not chopped up by a purely mechanical and irrational verse division, but divided according to a logical plan, will be of great help.

Having discovered the divisions of the book, proceed to give to each section an appropriate caption. Make this caption as precise a statement of the general contents of the section as possible. Make it also as terse and striking as possible, so that it will fix itself in the mind. As far as possible, let the captions of the subdivisions connect themselves with the general caption of the division. Do not attempt too elaborate a division at first. The following division of 1 Peter, without many marked subdivisions, will serve as a simple illustration of what is meant.

V. Example: 1 Peter

1. Chap. 1:1, 2. Introduction and salutation to the pilgrims and sojourners in Pontus, etc.

2. Chap. 1:3–12. The inheritance reserved in heaven and the salvation ready to be revealed for those pilgrims who in the midst of manifold temptations are kept by the power of God through faith.

3. Chap. 1:13–25. The pilgrim's conduct during the days of his pilgrimage.

4. Chap. 2:1–10. The high calling, position, and destiny of the pilgrim people.

5. Chap. 2:11, 12. The pilgrim's conduct during the days of his pilgrimage.

6. Chap. 2:13–17. The pilgrim's duty toward the human governments under which he lives.

7. Chap. 2:18–3:7. The duty of various classes of pilgrims.

   a. Chap. 2:18–25. The duty of servants toward their masters, enforced by an appeal to Christ's conduct under injustice and reviling.

   b. Chap. 3:1–6. The duty of wives toward husbands.

   c. Chap. 3:7. The duty of husbands toward their wives.

8. Chap. 3:8–12. The conduct of pilgrims toward one another.

9. Chap. 3:13–22. The pilgrim suffering for righteousness' sake.

10. Chap. 4:1–6. The pilgrim's separation from the practices of those among whom he spends the days of his pilgrimage.

11. Chap. 4:7–11. The pilgrim's sojourning drawing to a close, and his conduct during the last days.

12. Chap. 4:12–19. The pilgrim suffering for and with Christ.

13. Chap. 5:1–4. The duty and reward of elders.

14. Chap. 5:5–11. The pilgrim's walk—humble and trustful, watchful, and steadfast—and a doxology.

15. Chap. 5:12–14. Conclusion and benediction.

VI. Study Each Verse in Order

The fifth work is to take up each verse in order and study it.

1. How Do We Understand the Exact Meaning of the Verse?

The first thing to be done in this verse by verse study of the book is to get the exact meaning of the verse. How is this to be done? There are three steps that lead into the meaning of a verse.

A. Understand the Exact Meaning of Each Word

The first step is to get the exact meaning of the words used. There will be found two classes of words: those whose meaning is perfectly apparent, those whose meaning is doubtful. It is quite possible to find the precise meaning of these doubtful words. This is not done by consulting a dictionary. That is an easy but dangerous method of finding the scriptural significance of a word. The only safe and sure method is to study the usage of the word in the Bible itself, and especially in that particular Bible writer, one of whose writings we are studying.

To study the Bible usage of words one must have a concordance. Altogether, the best Concordance is Strong's *Exhaustive Concordance of the Bible.* The next best is Young's *Analytical Concordance.* Cruden's *Complete Concordance* will do, if one cannot afford a better. But the student should, as soon as possible, procure Strong's *Exhaustive Concordance.*

All the passages in which the word occurs, whose meaning is being sought, should be found and examined, and in this way the precise meaning of the word will be determined.

Many an important Bible doctrine turns upon the meaning of a word. Thus, for example, two schools of theology divide on the meaning of the word "justify." The critical question is, does the word "justify" mean "to make righteous," or does it mean "to count or declare righteous"? The correct interpretation of many passages of Scripture turns upon the sense which we give to this word.

Let one look up all the passages in the Bible in which the word is found, and there will be no doubt as to the Bible usage and meaning of the word. Deut. 25:1; Ex. 23:7; Is. 5:23; Luke 16:15; Rom. 2:13; 3:23, 24; Luke 18:14; and Rom. 4:2–8 RV, will serve to illustrate the biblical usage.

By the use of *Strong's* concordance, or *Young's,* the student will see that the same word may be used in the English version as the translation of several Greek or Hebrew words. Of course, in determining the biblical usage, we should give especial weight to those passages in which the English word examined is the translation of the same word in Greek or Hebrew. Either of the concordances just mentioned will enable us to do this, even though we are not at all acquainted with Greek or Hebrew. It will be much easier to do it with *Strong's* concordance than *Young's.*

It is surprising how many knotty problems in the interpretation of scripture are solved by the simple examination of the biblical usage of words. For example, one of the burning questions of today is the meaning of 1 Jn. 1:7. Does this verse teach that "the blood of Jesus Christ cleanseth us" from all the *guilt* of sin; or does it teach us that "the blood of Jesus Christ" cleanseth us from the *very presence of sin*, so that by the blood of Christ, indwelling sin is itself eradicated? Many of those who read this question will answer it offhand at once, one way or the other. But the off-hand way of answering questions of this kind is a very bad way.

Take your concordance and look up every passage in the Bible in which the word "cleanse" is used in connection with blood, and the question will be answered conclusively and forever. Never conclude that you have the right meaning of a verse until you have carefully determined the meaning of all doubtful words in it by an examination of Bible usage. Even when you are pretty sure you know the meaning of words, it is well not to be too sure until you have looked them up.

B. Carefully Look at the Context

The second step in ascertaining the meaning of a verse is to carefully notice the context: what goes before and what comes after. Many verses, if they stood alone, might be capable of several interpretations, but when what goes before and what comes after is considered, all the interpretations but one are seen to be impossible.

Take, for example, Jn. 14:18, "I will not leave you desolate: I come unto you." (RV) To what does Jesus refer when He says "I come unto you"? One commentator says, He refers to His reappearance to His disciples after His resurrection to comfort them. Another says that He refers to His second coming, as it is called. Another says He refers to His coming through the Holy Spirit's work to manifest Himself to His disciples and make His abode with them.

Which does He mean? When "doctors disagree," can an ordinary layman decide? Yes, very often. Surely in this case. If any one will carefully note what Jesus is talking about in the verses immediately preceding (verses 15–17) and in the verses immediately following (verses 19–26), he will have no doubt as to what coming Jesus refers to in this passage. You can see this by trying it for yourself.

A very large proportion of the vexed questions of biblical interpretation, can be settled by this very simple method of noticing what goes before and what comes after. Many of the sermons one hears become very absurd when one takes the trouble to notice the setting of the preacher's text and how utterly foreign the thought of the sermon is to the thought of the text, regarded in the light of the context.

C. Examine Parallel Passages

The third step in ascertaining the correct and precise meaning of a verse, is the examination of parallel passages, i.e., passages that treat the same subject—passages, for example, that give another account of the same address or event, or passages that are evidently intended as a commentary on the passage in hand. Very often, after having carefully studied the words used and the context, we will still be in doubt as to which of two or three possible interpretations of a verse is the one intended by the writer or speaker. In such a case there is always somewhere else in the Bible a passage that will settle this question.

Take for example, Jn. 14:3, "I come again and will receive you unto myself; that where I am, there ye may be also." (RV) A careful consideration of the words used in their relation to one another will go far in determining the meaning of this passage, but still we find among commentators whose opinion ought to have some weight, these four interpretations. First, the coming here referred to is Christ's coming at death to receive the believer unto himself, as in the case of Stephen. Second, the coming again at the resurrection. Third, the coming again through the Holy Spirit. Fourth, the coming again of Christ when He returns personally and gloriously at the end of the age.

Which of these four interpretations is the correct one? What has already been said about verse 18 might seem to settle the question, but it does not; for it is not at all clear that the coming in verse 3 is the same as in verse 18, for what is said in connection with the two comings is altogether different. In the one case, it is a coming of Christ to "receive you unto myself, that where I am, there ye may be also;" in the other case, it is a coming of Christ to manifest Himself unto us and make His abode with us. But fortunately there is a verse that settles the question, an inspired commentary on the Words of Jesus. This is found in 1 Thess. 4:16, 17. This will be seen clearly if we arrange the two passages in parallel columns.

John 14:3	1 Thess. 4:16, 17
I come again	The Lord himself shall descend
and will receive you unto myself	we. . .shall be caught up. . .to meet the Lord,
that where I am, there ye may be also.	so shall we ever be with the Lord.

The two passages manifestly match exactly in the three facts stated, and beyond a doubt refer to the same event. But if any one will look at all closely at 1 Thess. 4:16, 17, there can be no doubt as to what coming of our Lord is referred to there. *The Treasury of Scripture Knowledge* will be of great assistance in finding parallel passages.

These are the three steps that lead us into the meaning of a verse. They require work, but it is work that anyone can do, and when the meaning of a verse is thus settled, we arrive at conclusions that are correct and fixed. After taking these steps it is well to consult commentaries, and see how our conclusions agree with those of others.

Before we proceed to the next thing to be done with a verse after its meaning has been determined, let it be said, that God intended to convey some definite truth in each verse of scripture and any of one of from two to a dozen interpretations of a verse is not as good as another. With every verse of scripture we should ask, not, "What can this be made to teach?" but, "What was this intended to teach?" and we should not rest satisfied until we have settled that. Of course, it is admitted that a verse may have a primary meaning and other more remote meanings. For example, a prophecy may have its primary fulfillment in some personage or event near at hand, e. g., Solomon, and a more remote and complete fulfillment in Christ.

2. Analyze the Verse

We are not through with a verse when we have determined its meaning. The next thing to do is to analyze the verse. This is most interesting and profitable work. It is also a rare education of the various faculties of the intellect. The way to do it is this: Look steadfastly at the verse and ask yourself, "What does this verse teach?" Then, begin to write down: "This verse teaches, first,____; second,____; third,____," etc.

At the first glance, very likely, you will see but one or two things the verse teaches, but, as you look again and again, the teachings will begin to multiply, and you will wonder how one verse could teach so much, and you will have an ever growing sense of the divine authorship of the Book.

It is related of the younger Prof. Agassiz, that a young man came to him to study ichthyology. The Professor gave him a fish to study and told him to come back when he had mastered that fish and get another lesson. In time the young man came back and told Prof. A. what he had observed about the fish. When he had finished, to his surprise he was given the same fish again, and told to study it further. He came back again, having observed new facts, and, as he supposed, all the facts about the fish. But again he was given the same fish to study, and so it went on, lesson after lesson, until that student had been taught what his perceptive faculties were for, and also taught to do thorough work. In the same way ought we to study the Bible.

We ought to come back to the same verse of the Bible again and again, until we have gotten, as far as it is possible to us, all that is in the verse. Then the probability is that when we come back to the same verse several months afterward we will find something we did not see before. It may be, that an illustration of this method of analysis will be helpful. Let us take 1 Pet. 1:1, 2. (Here we have an instance in which the verse division of our Authorized version is so manifestly illogical and absurd that in our analysis we cannot follow it, but must take the two verses together. This will often be the case.)

VII. Example: 1 Peter 1:1, 2

These verses teach:

1. This epistle is by Peter.

2. The Peter who wrote this epistle was an apostle of Jesus Christ.

3. Peter delighted to think and speak of himself as one sent of Jesus Christ. (Compare 2 Pet. 1:1) *Note: apostle is Greek for Latin missionary.*

4. The name, Jesus Christ (which is used twice in these two verses). Significance:

   a. Savior.

   b. Anointed One.

   c. Fulfiller of the Messianic predictions of the Old Testament "Christ" has especial reference to the earthly reign of Christ.

5. This epistle was written to the elect, especially to the elect who are sojourners of the dispersion in Pontus, i.e., Paul's old field of labor. *Note: the question of whether speaking of the dispersion implies that the destination of this epistle was to Jewish Christians will have been taken up and answered in the introduction to the epistle.)*

6. Believers are:

   a. elect or chosen of God.

   b. foreknown of God.

   c. sanctified of the Spirit.

   d. sprinkled by the blood of Jesus Christ.

   e. sojourners or pilgrims on earth.

   f. subjects of multiplied grace.

   g. possessors of multiplied peace.

7. Election.
   a. Who are the elect? Believers. (Compare verse 5.)
   b. To what are they elect?
       1) Obedience.
       2) Sprinkling of the blood of Jesus.
           a) According to what are they elect? The fore-knowledge of God. (Compare Rom. 8:29, 30.)
           b) In what are they elect? Sanctification of the Spirit.
           c) The test of election: obedience. (Compare 2 Pet. 1:10.)
   c. The work of the three persons of the Trinity in election
       1) The Father foreknows.
       2) Jesus Christ cleanses from guilt by His blood.
       3) The Spirit sanctifies.

8. God is the Father of the elect.

9. The humanity of Christ: seen in the mention of His blood.

10. The reality of the body of Jesus Christ: seen in the mention of His blood.

11. It is by His blood and not by His example that Jesus Christ delivers from sin.

12. Peter's first and great wish and prayer for those to whom he wrote was that grace and peace might be multiplied.

13. It is not enough to have grace and peace. One should have multiplied grace and peace.

14. That men already have grace and peace is no reason to cease praying for them, but rather an incentive to prayer that they may have more grace and peace.

15. Grace precedes peace. (Compare all passages where these words are found together.)

This is simply an illustration of what is meant by analyzing a verse. The whole book should be gone through in this way.

There are three rules to be observed in this analytical work.

First. Do not put anything into your analysis that is not clearly in the verse. One of the greatest faults in Bible study is reading into passages what God never put into them. Some men have their pet doctrines, and see them everywhere, and even where God does not see them. No matter how true, precious or scriptural a doctrine is, do not put it into your analysis where it is not in the verse. Considerable experience with classes in this kind of study leads me to emphasize this rule.

Second. Find all that is in the verse. This rule can only be carried out relatively. Much will escape you, the verses of the Bible are such a great deep, but do not rest until you have dug, and dug, and dug, and there seems to be nothing more to find.

Third. State what you do find just as accurately and exactly as possible. Do not be content with putting into your analysis something like what is in the verse, but state in your analysis precisely what *is* in the verse.

VIII. Classify Your Results

The sixth work in the study of the book is to classify the results obtained by the verse by verse analysis. By your verse by verse analysis you have discovered and recorded a great number of facts. The work now is to get these facts into an orderly shape. To do this, go carefully through your analysis and note the subjects treated in the epistle. Write these subjects down as fast as they are noted.

Having made a complete list of the subjects treated in the book, write these subjects on separate cards or sheets of paper, and then, going through the analysis again, copy each point in the analysis upon its appropriate sheet of paper, e.g., every point regarding God the Father upon the card at the top of which this subject is written. This general classification should be followed by a more thorough and minute subdivision.

Suppose that we are studying the First Epistle of Peter. Having completed our analysis of the epistle, and gone over it carefully, we will find that the following subjects, at least, are treated in the epistle:

IX. Example: General Subjects Treated in I Peter

1. God
2. Jesus Christ
3. The Holy Spirit
4. The believer
5. Wives and husbands
6. Servants
7. The new birth
8. The Word of God
9. Old Testament Scripture
10. The prophets
11. Prayer
12. Angels
13. The devil
14. Baptism
15. The Gospel
16. Salvation
17. The World
18. Gospel preachers and teachers
19. Heaven
20. Humility
21. Love

These will serve for general headings. But after the material found in the analysis is arranged under these headings, it will be found to subdivide itself naturally into numerous subdivisions. For example, the material under the head "God" can be subdivided into these subdivisions:

X. Example: Some Detailed Topics Under "God"

1. His names. (The material under this head is quite rich.)

2. His attributes. This should be subdivided again: His holiness, His power, His foreknowledge, His faithfulness, His long-suffering, His grace (there are twenty-five or more points on God's grace in the epistle), His mercy, His impartiality, and His severity.

3. God's judgments.

4. God's will.

5. What is acceptable to God.

6. What is due to God.

7. God's dwelling place.

8. God's dominion.

9. God's work. What God does.

10. The things of God, e.g., "The mighty hand of God," "the house of God," "the gospel of God," "the flock of God," "the people of God," " the bond-servant of God," "the Word of God," "the oracles of God," etc., etc.

An illustration in full of the classified arrangement of the teaching of a book on one doctrine, will probably show better how to do this work than any abstract statement, and it will also illustrate in part how fruitful is this method of study. We will take 1 Peter again—its teaching regarding the believer.

XI. Example: What I Peter Teaches About the Believer

A. His privileges.

1. His election.

   a. He is foreknown of the Father, 1:2.

   b. He is elect or chosen of God, 1:1.

   c. He is chosen of God, according to His foreknowledge, 1:2.

   d. He is chosen unto obedience, 1:2.

   e. He is chosen unto the sprinkling of the blood of Jesus, 1:2.

   f. He is chosen in sanctification of the Spirit, 1:2.

2. His calling.

   a. By whom called:
      1) God, 1:15.
      2) The God of all grace, 5:10.

   b. To what called:
      1) The imitation of Christ in the patient taking of suffering for well doing, 2:20, 21.
      2) To render blessings for reviling, 3:9.
      3) Out of darkness into God's marvelous light, 2:9.
      4) To God's eternal glory, 5:10.

   c. In whom called: in Christ, 5:10.

   d. The purpose of his calling:
      1) That he may show forth the praises of Him who called, 2:9.
      2) That he may inherit a blessing, 3:9.

3. His regeneration. He has been begotten again:

   a. of God, 1:3.

   b. unto a living hope, 1:3.

    c.   unto an inheritance incorruptible, undefiled, that fadeth not away, reserved in Heaven, 1:4.

    d.   by the resurrection of Jesus Christ, 1:3.

    e.   of incorruptible seed by the word of God that liveth, etc., 1:23.

4.   His redemption. He has been redeemed:

    a.   not with corruptible things, as silver and gold, 1:18.

    b.   with precious blood, even the blood of Christ, 1:19.

    c.   from his vain manner of life, handed down from his fathers, 1:18.

    d.   his sins have been borne by Christ, in His own body, on the tree, 2:24.

5.   His sanctification: he is sanctified by the Spirit, 1:2.

6.   His cleansing: he is cleansed by the blood, 1; 2.

7.   His security.

    a.   He is guarded by the power of God, 1:5.

    b.   He is guarded unto a salvation ready, or prepared, to be revealed in the last time, 1:5.

    c.   God careth for him, 5:7.

    d.   He can cast all his anxiety upon God, 5:7.

    e.   The God of all grace will perfect, establish, strengthen him, after a brief trial of suffering, 5:10. RV.

    f.   None can harm him if he is zealous of that which is good, 3:13.

    g.   He shall not be put to shame, 2:6.

8.   His joy.

    a.   The character of his joy.

1) His present joy: a great joy, 1:8. RV; an unspeakable joy, 1:8; a joy full of glory, 1:8. *(Note: this present joy cannot be hindered by being put to grief, because of manifold temptations, 1:6.)*

2) His future joy: exceeding, 4:13.

b. In what he rejoices:

1) In the salvation prepared to be revealed in the last time, 1:6.

2) Because of his faith in the unseen Jesus Christ, 1:8.

3) In fellowship in Christ's sufferings, 4:13.

c. In what he shall rejoice: in the revelation of Christ's glory, 4:13. *Note: present joy in fellowship with the sufferings of Christ, is the condition of exceeding joy at the revelation of Christ's glory, 4:13.*

9. His hope.

a. Its character: a living hope, 1:3; a reasonable hope, 3:15; an inward hope, "in you," 3:15.

b. In whom is his hope: in God, 1:21.

c. The foundation of his hope: the resurrection of Jesus Christ, 1:3–21.

10. His salvation.

a. A past salvation: has been redeemed, 1:18–19; has been healed, 2:24. *Note: by baptism, after a true likeness, the believer, as Noah by the flood, has passed out of the old life of nature into the new resurrection life of grace, 3:21.*

b. A present salvation: he is now receiving the salvation of his soul, 1:9.

c. A growing salvation, through feeding on His word, 2:2 RV.

d. A future salvation: ready or prepared to be revealed in the last time, 1:5.

11. The believer's possessions.
    a. God as his Father, 1:17.
    b. Christ as his:
       1) sin bearer, 2:24.
       2) example, 2:21.
       3) fellow sufferer, 4:13.
    c. A living hope, 1:3.
    d. An incorruptible, undefiled, unfading inheritance reserved in heaven, 1:4.
    e. Multiplied grace and peace, 1:2.
    f. Spiritual milk without guile for his food, 2:2.
    g. Gifts for service—each believer has, or may have, some gift, 4:10.

12. What believers are.
    a. An elect race, 2:9.
    b. A royal priesthood, 2:9.
    c. A holy priesthood, 2:5.
    d. A holy nation, 2:9.
    e. A people for God's own possession, 2:9 RV.
    f. Living stones, 2:5.
    g. The house of God, 4:17.
    h. A spiritual house, 2:5.
    i. The flock of God, 5:2.
    j. Children of obedience, 1:14 RV.
    k. Partakers of, or partners in, Christ's suffering, 4:13.
    l. Partakers of, or partners in, the glory to be revealed, 5:1.

    m.   Sojourners or strangers, 1:1.

    n.   Foreigners on earth: he has no civil rights here: his citizenship is in heaven, 2, 11. (Compare Phil. 3:20 RV.)

    o.   A sojourner on his way to another country, 2:1.

    p.   A Christian: representative of Christ, 4:16.

13.   The believer's possibilities.

    a.   He may die unto sin, 2:24.

    b.   He may live unto righteousness, 2:24. *Note: we must die unto sin if we are to live unto righteousness, 2:24.*

    c.   He may follow in Christ's steps, 2:21.

    d.   He may cease from sin, 4:1.

    e.   He may cease from living to the lusts of men, 4:2.

    f.   He may live unto the will of God, 4:2. *Note: it is through suffering in the flesh that he ceases from sin and living to the lusts of men, and lives to the will of God.*

14.   What was for the believer.

    a.   The ministry of the prophets was in his behalf, 1:12.

    b.   The preciousness of Jesus is for him, 2:7 RV.

15.   Unclassified.

    a.   Has the gospel preached to him in the Holy Ghost, 1:12.

    b.   Grace is to be brought unto him at the revelation of Jesus Christ, 1:3. (Compare Eph. 3:7.)

    c.   Has tasted that the Lord is gracious, 2:3.

B. The believer's trial and sufferings.

1.   The fact of the believer's sufferings and trials, 1:6.

2.   The nature of the believer's sufferings and trials.

    a.   He endures griefs, suffering wrongfully, 2:19.

    b.   He suffers for righteousness' sake, 3:14.

    c.   He suffers for well doing, 3:17; 2:20.

    d.   He suffers as a Christian, 4:16.

    e.   He is subjected to manifold temptations, 1:6.

    f.   He is put to grief in manifold temptations, 1:6.

    g.   He is spoken against as an evil doer, 2:12.

    h.   His good manner of life is reviled, 3:16.

    i.   He is spoken evil of because of his separated life, 4:4.

    j.   He is reproached for the name of Christ, 4, 14.

    k.   He is subjected to fiery trials, 4:12.

3.   Encouragements for believers undergoing fiery trials and suffering.

    a.   It is better to suffer for well doing than for evil doing, 3:17.

    b.   Judgment must begin at the House of God, and the present judgment of believers through trial is not comparable to the future end of those who obey not the gospel, 4:17.

    c.   Blessed is the believer who does suffer for righteousness' sake, 3:14. (Compare Matt. 5:10–12.)

    d.   Blessed is the believer who is reproached for the name of Christ, 4:14.

    e.   The Spirit of Glory and the Spirit of God rests upon the believer who is reproached for the name of Christ, 4:14.

    f.   The believer's grief is for a little while, 1:6 RV.

    g.   The believer's suffering is for a little while, 5:10. RV.

    h.   Suffering for a little while will be followed by God's glory in Christ, which is eternal, 5:10.

i.   The suffering endured for a little while is for the testing of faith, 1:7.

j.   The fiery trial is for a test, 4:12.

k.   The faith thus proved is more precious than gold, 1:7.

l.   Faith proven by manifold temptations will be found unto praise, and honor, and glory, at the revelation of Jesus Christ, 1:7.

m.   It is that his proved faith may be found unto praise and glory and honor at the revelation of Jesus Christ, that the believer is for a little while subjected to manifold temptations, 1:7.

n.   It is pleasing to God when a believer, for conscience toward God, endures grief, suffering wrongfully, 2:19 RV.

o.   It is pleasing to God when a believer takes it patiently, when he does well and suffers for it, 2:20.

p.   Through suffering in the flesh we cease from sin, 4:1.

q.   Those who speak evil of us shall give account to God, 4:5.

r.   Sufferings are being shared by fellow believers, 5:9.

s.   Christ suffered for us, 2:21.

t.   Christ suffered for sins once (or once for all), the righteous for the unrighteous, that He might bring us to God, being put to death in the flesh, but quickened in the spirit, 3:18.

u.   Christ left the believer an example that he should follow in His steps, 2:21.

v.   In our fiery trials we are made partakers of, or partakers in, Christ's sufferings, 4:13.

w.   When His glory is revealed we shall be glad also with exceeding joy, 4:13.

4. How the believer should meet his trial and sufferings.

    a. The believer should not regard his fiery trial as a strange thing, 4:12.

    b. The believer should expect fiery trial, 4:12.

    c. When the believer suffers as a Christian, let him not be ashamed, 4:16.

    d. When the believer suffers as a Christian, let him glorify God in this name, 4:16.

    e. When the believer suffers fiery trials he should rejoice, insomuch as he is made partaker of Christ's suffering, 4:13 RV.

    f. When the believer suffers, let him not return reviling with reviling, or suffering with threatening; but commit himself to Him that judgeth righteously, 2:23.

    g. When the believer suffers, he should in well-doing commit the keeping of his soul unto God, as unto a faithful Creator, 4:19.

C. The believer's dangers.

1. The believer may fall into fleshly lusts that war against the soul, 2:11.

2. The believer may sin, 2:20 RV.

3. The believer may fall into sins of the gravest character, 4:15. (*Note in this verse the awful possibilities that lie dormant in the heart of at least a sincere professed believer.*)

4. The believer's prayers may be hindered, 3:7.

5. The believer is in danger that his high calling and destiny tempt him to despise human laws and authority, 2:13.

6. The believer is in danger that his high calling lead him to lose sight of his lowly obligations to human masters, 2:18.

7. Young believers are in danger of disregarding the will and authority of old believers. 5:15.

D. The believer's responsibility.

1. Each believer has an individual responsibility, 4:10 RV.

2. Each believer's responsibility is for the gift he has received, 4:10.

E. The believer's duties.

1. What the believer should be.

    a. Be holy in all manner of living: because God is holy, 1:15; because it is written "ye shall be holy," 1:16. RV.

    b. Be like Him who called him, 1:15–16.

    c. Be sober, (or of a calm, collected, thoughtful spirit,) 1:13; 4:7; 5:8.

    d. Be sober, or of a calm, collected, thoughtful spirit *unto prayer*, 4:7.

    e. Be of a sound mind: because the end of all things is approaching, 4:7.

    f. Be watchful, 5:8.

    g. Be steadfast in the faith, 5:9.

    h. Be subject to every ordinance of man.
       1) For the Lord's sake, 2:13.
       2) To the King, as supreme, 2:13.
       3) To governors, as sent by the King for the punishment of evil doers, and for praise to them that do well, 2:14.
       4) Because this is God's will, 2:15.

    i. Be like-minded, 3:8.

    j. Be sympathetic, 3:8.

    k. Be tenderhearted, 3:8.

l.   Be humble minded, 3:8.

m. Be ready:
   1) Always.
   2) To give an answer to every man that asketh a reason of the hope that is in him.
   3) With meekness and fear.
   4) In order to put to shame those who revile their good manner of life in Christ, 3:16.

n. Should not be troubled, 3:14.

2. What the believer should *not* do.

   a. The believer should not fashion himself according to the lusts of the old life of ignorance, 1:14.

   b. The believer should not render evil for evil, 3:9.

   c. The believer should not render reviling for reviling, 3:9.

   d. The believer should not fear the world's fear, 3:14.

   e. The believer should not live his remaining time in the flesh to the lusts of men, 4:2.

3. What the believer *should* do.

   a. He should live as a child of obedience, 1:14.

   b. Pass the time of his sojourning here in fear, 1:17.

   c. Abstain from fleshly lusts that war against the soul, 2:11.

   d. Observe God's will as the absolute law of life, 2:15.

   e. Let his conscience be governed by the thought of God and not by the conduct of men, 2:19.

   f. Sanctify Christ in his heart as Lord, 3:15 RV. (Compare Is. 8:13.)

   g. Live his remaining time in the flesh to the will of God, 4:2.

h. Put away:
    1) All malice, 2:1.
    2) All guile, 2:1.
    3) Hypocrisies, 2:1.
    4) Envies, 2:1.
    5) All evil speaking, 2:1.

i. Come unto the Lord as unto a living stone, 2:4.

j. Show forth the excellencies of him who called him out of darkness into His marvelous light, 2:9.

k. Arm himself with the mind of Christ: i.e. to suffer in the flesh, 4:1.

l. Cast all his care upon God because he careth for him, 5:7.

m. Stand fast in the true grace of God, 5:12.

n. Withstand the devil, 5:9.

o. Humble himself under the mighty hand of God, 5:5.
    1) Because God resisteth the proud and giveth grace unto the humble, 5:5–6.
    2) That God may exalt him in due time, 5:6.

p. Glorify God when he suffers as a Christian, 4:16.

q. See to it that he does not suffer as a thief or as an evil doer or as a meddler in other men's matters, 4:15.

r. Rejoice in fiery trial, 4:13.

s. Attitudes and behavior towards various persons:
    1) Toward God—fear, 2:17.
    2) Toward the King—honor, 2:17.
    3) Toward masters—be in subjection with all fear (not only to the good and gentle, but to the forward) 2:18.
    4) Toward the brotherhood:
        a) Love, 2:17; 1:22; 4:8.

b) Love from the heart, 1:22 RV.

c) Love fervently—intensely, 1:22; 4:8.

d) Gird themselves with humility as with a slave's apron, unto one another. i.e.: first, be one another's slaves; second, wear humility as a token of their readiness to serve one another, 5:5. (Compare Jn. 13:4–5.)

e) Minister the gift he has received from God among the brethren as a good steward of the manifold grace of God, 4:10.

f) Use hospitality one to another without murmuring, 4:9.

g) Salute one another with a holy kiss, 5:14.

5) Toward his revilers: render blessing for reviling, 3:9.

6) Toward the Gentiles: have his behavior seemly among the Gentiles, 2:12. Notes—*First. The reason why he should have his behavior seemly among the Gentiles; that the Gentiles might glorify God in the day of visitation, 2:12. Second. This seemly behavior should consist in good works which the Gentiles could behold, 2:12.*

7) Toward foolish men: by well doing put to silence their ignorance, 2:15.

8) Toward all men—honor, 2:17. *Note: the especial duties of believing husbands and wives, toward one another, comes under a special classification.*

t. Long for the sincere milk of the word, 2:2.

u. Gird up the loins of his mind, 1:13.

v. Grow, 2:2.

w. Set his hope perfectly on the grace to be brought unto him at the revelation of Jesus Christ, 1:13 RV.

F. The believer's characteristics

1. His faith and hope is in God, 1:21.

2. Believes in God through Jesus Christ, 1:21.

3. Calls on God as Father, 1:17.

4. Believes in Christ, though he has never seen Him, 1:8.

5. Lives Christ though he has never seen Him, 1:8.

6. Is returned unto the Shepherd and Bishop of his soul, 2:25.

7. Has purified his soul in obedience to the truth, 1:22.

8. Has unfeigned love for the brethren, 1:22.

9. Has a good manner of life, 3:16.

10. Does not run with the Gentiles among whom he lives to the same excess of riot (lives a separated life), 4:4.

11. Refrains his tongue from evil. 3:10. Refrains his lips that they speak not guile, 3:10.

12. Turns away from evil, 3:11.

13. Does good, 3:11.

14. Seeks peace, 3:11.

15. Pursues peace, 3:11.

Note: from 11 to 14 would very properly come under duties.

G. The believer's warfare.

1. The believer has a warfare before him, 4:1.

2. The mind of Christ is the proper armament for this warfare, 4:1.

3. The warfare is with the devil, 5:8–9.

4. Victory is possible for the believer, 5:9.

5. Victory is won through steadfastness in the faith, 5:9.

XII. Meditate Upon and Digest the Results

We come now to the seventh and last work. This is simply to meditate upon, and so digest, the results obtained. At first thought it might seem that when we had completed our classification of results our work was finished, but this is not so. These results are for use: first, for personal enjoyment and appropriation, and afterward to give out to others.

The appropriation of results is effected by meditation upon them. We are no more through with a book when we have carefully and fully classified its contents than we are through with a meal when we have it arranged in an orderly way upon the table. It is there to eat, digest and assimilate. One of the great failures in much of the Bible study of the day is just at this point. There is observation, analysis, classification, but no meditation.

There is perhaps nothing so important in Bible study as meditation. (See Josh. 1:8; Ps. 1:2, 3.) Take your classified teachings and go slowly over them, and ponder them, point by point, until these wonderful truths live before you and sink into your soul, and live in you, and become part of your life. Do this again and again. Nothing will go further than meditation to make one great and fresh and original as a thinker and speaker. Very few people in this world *think.*

The method of study outlined in this chapter can be shortened to suit the time and industry of the student. For example, one can omit the fifth work (Step 5), and proceed at once to go through the book as a whole, and note down its teachings on different doctrines. This will greatly shorten and lighten the work. It will also greatly detract from the richness of the results, it will not be as thorough; as accurate or as scholarly; and will not be nearly so good a mental discipline. But many people are lazy, and everybody is in a hurry. So if you will not follow out the fuller plan, the shorter is suggested. But any man can be, if he will, a scholar at least in the most important line—that of biblical study.

A still briefer plan of book study and yet very profitable, if one has not time for anything better, is to do the second work (Step 2) and then go through the Epistle verse by verse, looking up all the references given in *The Treasury of Scripture Knowledge.* But we urge every reader to try the full method described in this chapter with at least one short book in the Bible.

CHAPTER 3

Topical Study

A second method of Bible study is the topical method. This consists in searching through the Bible to find out what its teaching is on various topics. It is perhaps the most fascinating method of Bible study. It yields the largest immediate results, though not the largest ultimate results.

It has advantages. The only way to master any topic is to go through the Bible and find what it has to teach on that topic. Almost any great subject will take a remarkable hold upon the heart of a Christian man, if he will take time to go through the Bible, from Genesis to Revelation, and note what it has to say on that topic. He will have a more full and more correct understanding of that topic than he ever had before.

It is said of Mr. Moody, that many years ago he took up the study of "grace" in this way. Day after day he went through the Bible, studying what it had to say about "grace." As the Bible doctrine unfolded before his mind, his heart began to burn, until at last, full of the subject and on fire with the subject, he ran out on to the street, and, taking hold of the first man he met, he said: "Do you know grace?" "Grace who?" was the reply. "The grace of God that bringeth salvation." Then he just poured out his soul on that subject.

If any child of God will study "grace," or "love," or "faith," or "prayer," or any other great Bible doctrine in that way, his soul too will become full of it. Jesus evidently studied the Old Testament scriptures in this way, for we read that "beginning at Moses and all the prophets, He expounded unto them in all the scriptures the things concerning Himself." (Luke 24:27) This method of study made the hearts of the two who walked with Him to burn within them. (Luke 24:32) Paul seems to have followed his Master in this method of study and teaching. (Acts 17:2, 3)

But the method has its dangers. Its very fascination is a danger. Many are drawn by the fascination of this method of study to give up all other methods of study, and this is a great misfortune.

A well-rounded, thorough-going knowledge of the Bible is not possible by this method of study. No one method of study will answer, if one desires to be a well-rounded and well-balanced Bible student. But the greatest danger lies in this, that every man is almost certain to have some line of topics in which he is especially interested, and if he studies his Bible topically, unless he is warned, he is more than likely to go over certain topics again and again, and be very strong in this line of truth, but other topics of equal importance he neglects, and thus becomes a one-sided man. We never know one truth correctly until we know it in its proper relations to other truths.

I know of people, for example, who are interested in the great doctrine of the Lord's second coming, and pretty much all their Bible studies are on that line. Now this is a precious doctrine, but there are other doctrines in the Bible which a man needs to know, and it is folly to study this doctrine alone.

I know others whose whole interest and study seems to center in the subject of "divine healing." It is related of one man that he confided to a friend that he had devoted his time for years to the study of the number "seven" in the Bible. This last is doubtless an extreme case, but it illustrates the danger in topical study.

It is certain that we never master the whole range of Bible truth if we pursue the topical method alone. A few rules concerning topical study will probably be helpful to most of the readers of this book.

I. Be Systematic

Be systematic. Do not follow your fancy in the choice of topics. Do not just take up any topic that happens to suggest itself. Make a list of all the subjects that you can think of that are touched upon in the Bible. Make it as comprehensive and complete as possible. Then take these topics up one by one in logical order. The following list of subjects is given as a suggestion. Each one can add to the list for himself and subdivide the general subjects into proper subdivisions.

II. List of Study Topics

God

God as a spirit.
The unity of God.
The eternity of God.
The omnipresence of God.
The personality of God.
The omnipotence of God.
The omniscience of God.
The holiness of God.
The love of God.
The righteousness of God.
The mercy or loving kindness of God.
The faithfulness of God.
The grace of God.

Jesus Christ

The divinity of Christ.
The subordination of Jesus Christ to the Father.
The human nature of Jesus Christ.
The character of Jesus Christ.

His holiness.
His love to God.
His love to man.
His love for souls.
His compassion.
His prayerfulness.
His meekness and humility.
The death of Jesus Christ.
The purpose of Christ's death.
Why did Christ die?
For whom did Christ die?
The results of Christ's death.
The resurrection of Jesus Christ.
The fact of the Resurrection.
The results of the Resurrection.
The importance of the Resurrection.
The manner of the Resurrection.
The ascension and exaltation of Jesus Christ.
The return or coming again of Jesus Christ.
The fact of His coming again.
The manner of His coming again.
The purpose of His coming again.
The results of His coming again.
The time of His coming again.
The reign of Jesus Christ.

The Holy Spirit

Personality of the Holy Spirit.
Deity of the Holy Spirit.
Distinction of the Holy Spirit from God the Father, and the Son, Jesus
Christ.
The subordination of the Holy Spirit to the Father and to the Son.
Names of the Holy Spirit.
The work of the Holy Spirit:
In the Universe.

In man in general.
In the believer.
In the prophet and apostle.
In Jesus Christ.

Man

His original condition.

His fall.

The present standing before God and present condition of man outside of the redemption that is in Jesus Christ.

The future destiny of those who reject the redemption that is in Jesus
Christ.

Justification.

The new birth.

Adoption.

The believer's assurance of salvation.

The flesh.

Sanctification.

Cleansing.

Consecration.

Faith.

Repentance.

Prayer.

Thanksgiving.

Praise.

Worship.

Love to God.

Love to Jesus Christ.

Love to man.

The future destiny of believers.

Angels

Their nature and position.

Their number.

Their abode.

Their character.
Their work.
Their destiny.

Satan or the Devil

His existence.
His nature and position.
His abode.
His work.
Our duty regarding him.
His destiny.

Demons

Their existence.
Their nature.
Their work.
Their destiny.

For a student who has the perseverance to carry it though, it might be recommended, to begin with the first topic on a list like this, and go right through it to the end, searching for everything the Bible has to say on these topics. This the author of this book has done, and thereby, gained a fuller knowledge of truth along these lines, and an immeasurably more vital grasp of the truth, than he ever obtained by somewhat extended studies in systematic theology. Many, however, will stagger at the *seeming* immensity of the undertaking. To such it is recommended to begin by selecting those topics that seem more important. But sooner or later, settle down to a thorough study of what the Bible has to teach about God and man. The "Abstract of Subjects, Doctrinal and Practical," in the back of *The Bible Text Cyclopedia* [by James Inglis] is very suggestive.

III. Be Thorough

Be thorough. Whenever you are studying any topic, do not be content with examining *some* of the passages in the Bible that bear upon the subject, but find, as far as possible, *every passage in the Bible that bears on this subject.* As long as there is a single passage in the Bible on any subject that you have not considered, you have not yet gotten a thoroughly true knowledge of that subject. How can we find all the passages in the Bible that bear on a subject?

First: by the use of the concordance. Look up every passage that has the word in it. Then look up every passage that has synonymous words in it. If, for example, you are studying the subject of prayer, look up every passage that has the word "pray" and its derivatives in it, and also every passage that has such words as "cry," "call," "ask," "supplication," "intercession," etc., in it.

Second: by the use of a Bible textbook. A test book arranges the passages of Scripture, not by the words used, but by the subjects treated, and there is many a verse, for example, on prayer, that does not have the word "prayer" or any synonymous word in it. Incomparably the best Bible text book is Inglis' *The Bible Text Cyclopedia.*

Third: passages not discovered by the use of either concordance or text book will come to light as we study by books, or as we read the Bible through in course, and so our treatment of topics will be ever broadening.

IV. Be Exact

Be exact. Get the exact meaning of each passage considered. Study each passage in its connection, and find its meaning in the way suggested in the chapter on "Study of Individual Books." Topical study is frequently carried on in a very slip-shod fashion. Passages, torn from their connection, are strung or huddled together because of some superficial connection with one another, and without much regard to their real sense and teaching, and this is called "topical study." This has brought the whole method of topical study into disrepute. But it is possible to be as exact and scholarly in topical study as in any other method, and when we are the results will be instructive and gratifying, and not misleading. But the results are sure to be misleading and unsatisfactory if the work is done in a careless, inexact way.

V. Classify and Write Down Your Results

Classify and write down your results. In the study of any large subject one will get together a great mass of matter. Having gotten it, it must now be gotten into shape. As you look it over carefully, you will soon see the facts that belong together. Arrange them together in a logical order. An illustrative topical study is given below: what the Bible teaches concerning the deity of Jesus Christ.

VI. Example: Jesus Christ: His Deity

1. Divine Names

A. Luke 22:70. "The Son of God." This name is given to Christ forty times. Besides this the synonymous expression "His son," "My son," are of frequent occurrence. That this name as used of Christ is a distinctly divine name appears from Jn. 5:18.

B. John 1:18. "The only begotten Son." This occurs five times. It is evident that the statement, that "Jesus Christ is the Son of God only in the same sense that all men are sons of God" is not true. Compare Mark 12:6. Here Jesus Himself, having spoken of all the prophets as servants of God, speaks of Himself as "one," "a beloved Son."

C. Rev. 1:17. "The first and the last." Compare Is. 41:4; 44:6. In these latter passages it is "Jehovah," "Jehovah of hosts," who is "the first and the last."

D. Rev. 22:12, 13, 16. First, "the Alpha and Omega." Second, "the beginning and the ending." In Rev. 1:8 RV, it is the Lord God who is the Alpha and Omega.

E. Acts 3:14. "The Holy One." In Hosea 11:9, and many other passages, it is God who is "the Holy One."

F. Mal. 3:1; Luke 2:11; Acts 9:17; Jn. 20:28; Heb. 1:11. "The Lord." This name or title is used of Jesus several hundred times. The word translated "Lord" is used in the New Testament in speaking of men nine times, e.g., Acts 16:30, Eph. 4:1, Jn. 12:21, but not at all in the way in which it used of Christ. He is spoken of as "the Lord" just as God is, compare Acts 4:26 with 4:33. Note also Matt. 22:43–45, Phil. 2:21, Eph. 4:5. If any one doubts the attitude of the apostles of Jesus toward Him as divine, they would do well to read one after another the passages which speak of Him as Lord.

G. Acts 10:36. "Lord of all."

H. 1 Cor. 2:8. "The Lord of Glory." In Ps. 24:8–10, it is "the Lord of Hosts" who is the King of Glory.

I. Is. 9:6. "Wonderful" (compare Judges 13:18 RV): "Mighty God": "Father of Eternity" (see RV margin.)

J. Heb. 1:8. "God." In Jn. 20:28, Thomas calls Jesus "my God," and is gently rebuked for not believing it before.

K. Matt. 1:23. "God with us."

L. Tit. 2:13 RV "Our great God."

M. Rom. 9:5. "God blessed forever."

Proposition: Sixteen names clearly implying deity are used of Christ in the Bible, some of them over and over again, the total number of passages reaching far into the hundreds.

2. Divine Attributes

A. Omnipotence.

1) Luke 4:39. Jesus has power over disease; it is subject to His word.

2) Luke 7:14–15; 8:54–55; Jn. 5:25. The Son of God has power over death, it is subject to His word.

3) Matt. 8:26–27. Jesus has power over the winds and sea, they are subject to His word.

4) Matt. 8:16; Luke 4:35, 36, 41. Jesus, the Christ, the Son of God, has power over demons, they are subject to His word.

5) Eph. 1:20–23. Christ is far above *all* principality and power and might, and dominion and every name that is named,

not only in this world, but also in that which is to come. All things are in subjection (RV), under His feet. All the hierarchies of the angelic world are under Him.

6) Heb. 1:3. The Son of God upholds *all* things by the word of His power.

Proposition. Jesus Christ, the Son of God, is omnipotent.

B. Omniscience.

1) Jn. 4:16–19. Jesus knows men's lives, even their secret history.

2) Mark 2:8; Luke 5:22; Jn. 2:24–25; Acts 1:24. Jesus knows the secret thoughts of men. He knew all men. He knew what was in man. (Compare to 2 Chron. 6:30; Jer. 17:9, 10. Here we see that God "only knoweth the hearts of the children of men.")

3) Jn. 6:64. Jesus knew from the beginning that Judas would betray Him. Not only men's present thoughts but their future choices were known to Him.

4) Jn. 1:48. Jesus knew what men were doing at a distance.

5) Luke 22:10, 12; Jn. 13:1; Luke 5:4–6. Jesus knew the future regarding not only God's acts, but regarding the minute specific acts of men, and even the fishes of the sea. *Note: many, if not all, of these items of knowledge up to this point could possibly, if they stood alone, be accounted for by saying that the Omniscient God revealed these specific things to Jesus.*

6) Jn. 21:17, 16:30; Col. 2:3. Jesus knew all things, in Him are hid all the treasures of wisdom and knowledge.

Proposition. Jesus Christ is omniscient.

Note: there was, as we shall see when we study the humanity of Christ, a voluntary veiling and abnegation of the exercise of His inherent divine omniscience. (Mark 11:12–14; Phil. 2:7)

C.   Omnipresence.

1)   Matt. 18:20. Jesus Christ is present in every place where two or three are gathered together in His name.

2)   Matt. 28:20. Jesus Christ is present with every one who goes forth into any part of the world to make disciples, etc.

3)   Jn. 3:13. The Son of man was in heaven while He was here on earth. *Note: this text is doubtful. (See* RV *and the* Variorum Bible.)

4)   Jn. 14:20; 2 Cor. 13:5. Jesus Christ is in each believer.

5)   Eph. 1:23. Jesus Christ filleth all in all.

Proposition. Jesus Christ is omnipresent.

D.   Eternity. Jn. 1:1; Mic. 5:2; Col. 1:17; Is 9:6; Jn 17:5; Jn. 6:62; Jn. 8:58; 1 Jn. 1:1, 27; Heb. 13:8.

Proposition. The Son of God was from all eternity.

E.   Immutability.

1)   Heb. 13:8; 1:12. Jesus Christ is unchangeable. He not only always is, but always is *the same.*

2)   Phil. 2:6. Jesus Christ before His incarnation was in the form of God. *Note: "morphe," translated "form," means "the form by which a person or thing strikes the vision; the external appearance." (Thayer,* Grk-Eng. Lexicon of the New Testament)

3)   Col. 2:9. In Christ dwelleth all the fullness of the Godhead in a bodily way.

Proposition. Five or more distinctively divine attributes are ascribed to Jesus Christ, and all the fullness of the Godhead is said to dwell in Him.

3. **Divine Offices**

   A. Creation. Heb. 1:10; Jn. 1:3; Col. 1:16. The Son of God, the eternal Word, the Lord, is creator of all created things.

   B. Preservation. Heb 1:3. The Son of God is the preserver of all things.

   C. The forgiveness of sin. Mark 2:5–10; Luke 7:48–50. Jesus Christ had power on earth to forgive sins. *Note: He taught that sins were sins against Himself. Luke 7:40–47: both Simon and the woman as sinners were debtors to Him, but in Ps. 51:4 sin is seen to be against God and God only.*

   D. Raising of the dead. Jn. 6:39–44; 5:28–29. It is Jesus Christ who raises the dead. *Question: Did not Elijah and Elisha raise the dead? No; God raised the dead in answer to their prayer, but Jesus Christ will raise the dead by His own word. During the days of His humiliation it was by prayer that Christ raised the dead. Jn. 11:41.*

   E. Transformation of bodies. Phil. 3:21 RV. Jesus Christ shall fashion anew the body of our humiliation into the likeness of His own glorious body.

   F. Judgment. 2 Tim. 4:1 RV. Christ Jesus shall judge the quick and the dead. *Note: Jesus Himself emphasized the divine character of this office. (Jn. 5:22–23)*

   G. The bestowal of eternal life. Jn. 10:28; 17, 2. Jesus Christ is the bestower of eternal life.

Proposition. Seven distinctively divine offices are predicated of Jesus Christ.

4. Use of the name of Jehovah God in the Old Testament and of Jesus Christ in the New Testament

Statements which in the Old Testament are made distinctly of Jehovah God are then taken in the New Testament to refer to Jesus Christ.

Old Testament	New Testament
Ps. 102:24–27	Heb. 1:10–12
Is. 40, 3–4	Matt. 3:3, Luke 1:68, 69, 76
Jer. 11:20; 17, 10	Rev. 11:23
Is. 60:19, Zech. 2:5	Luke 2:32
Is. 6:1; 3:10	Jn. 12:37–41
Is 8:13–14	1 Pet. 2:7–8
Is. 8:12–13	1 Pet. 3:14–15 RV
Num. 21:6–7	1 Cor. 10, 9. (See RV.)
Ps. 23:1; Is. 40:10–11	Jn. 10:11
Ez. 34:11; 12:16	Luke 19:10

"Lord" in the Old Testament always refers to God, except when the context clearly indicates otherwise. "Lord" in the New Testament always refers to Jesus Christ except where the context clearly indicates otherwise.

Proposition. Many statements which in the Old Testament are made distinctly of Jehovah God are taken in the New Testament to refer to Jesus Christ, i.e., in New Testament thought and doctrine, Jesus Christ occupies the place that Jehovah occupies in Old Testament thought and doctrine.

135

5. **The names of God the Father and Jesus Christ the Son**

The way in which the name of God the Father and Jesus Christ the Son are coupled together.

    A.   2 Cor. 13:14.

    B.   Matt. 28:19.

    C.   1 Thess. 3:11.

    D.   1 Cor. 12:4–6.

    E.   Tit. 3:4,5; compare Tit. 2:13.

    F.   Rom. 1:7. (Many instances of this sort: see all the Pauline epistles).

    G.   Jas. 1:1.

    H.   Jn. 14:23, "we," i.e., God the Father and I.

    I.   2 Pet. 1:1. (Compare RV.)

    J.   Col. 2:2. (See RV.)

    K.   Jn. 17:3.

    L.   Jn. 14:1, compare Jer. 17:5–7.

    M.   Rev. 7:10.

    N.   Rev. 5:13; compare Jn. 5:23.

Proposition. The name of Jesus Christ is coupled with that of God the Father in numerous passages in a way in which it would be impossible to couple the name of any finite being with that of the Deity.

6. **Divine worship to be given to Jesus Christ.**

    A.   Matt. 28:9; Luke 24:52; Matt. 14:33, compare Acts 10:25–26; Rev. 22:8–9; Matt. 4:9–10. Jesus Christ accepted without hesitation a worship which good men and angels declined with fear (horror). *Question: is not the verb translated "worship" in these passages used of reverence paid to men in high position? Yes; but not in this way by worshipers of Jehovah, as is seen by the way in which*

Peter and the angel drew back with horror when such worship was offered to them.

B.   1 Cor. 1:2; 2 Cor. 12:8,9; Acts 7:59 RV. Prayer is to be made to Christ.

C.   Ps. 45:11; Jn. 5:23; compare Rev. 5:8, 9, 12, 13. It is God the Father's will that all men pay the same divine honor to the Son as to Himself.

D.   Heb. 1:6; Phil, 2:10, 11; compare Is. 45:21, 23. The Son of God, Jesus, is to be worshiped as God by angels and men.

Proposition. Jesus Christ is a person to be worshiped by angels and men even as God the Father is worshiped.

VII. General Proposition

By the use of numerous divine names; by the ascription of all the distinctively divine attributes; by the predication of several divine offices; by referring statements which in the Old Testament distinctly name Jehovah God as their subject to Jesus Christ in the New Testament; by coupling the name of Jesus Christ with that of God the Father in a way in which it would be impossible to couple that of any finite being with that of the Deity; and by the clear teaching that Jesus Christ should be worshiped even as God the Father is worshiped—in all these unmistakable ways, God in His word distinctly proclaims that Jesus Christ is a divine being—is God.

One suggestion remains to be made in regard to topical study: get further topics for topical study from your book studies.

CHAPTER 4

Biographical Study

A third method of study is the *biographical*. This needs no definition. It consists in taking up the various persons mentioned in Scripture and studying their life, work and character. It is really a special form of topical study. It can be made very interesting and instructive. It is especially useful to the minister with a view to sermon building, but is profitable for all Christians. The following suggestions will help those who are not already experienced in this line of work.

1. Collect all the passages in the Bible in which the person to be studied is mentioned.

This is readily done by turning in *Strong's Concordance* to the person's name, and you will find every passage in which he or she, is mentioned given.

2. Analyze the character of the person.

This will require a repeated reading of the passages in which he is mentioned. This should be done with pencil in hand, that any characteristic may be noted down at once.

3. Note the elements of power and success.

4. Note the elements of weakness and failure.

5. Note the difficulties overcome.

6. Note the helps to success.

7. Note the privileges abused.

8. Note the opportunities neglected.

9. Note the opportunities improved.

10. Note the mistakes made.

11. Note the perils avoided.

12. Make a sketch of the life in hand.

Make it as vivid, living, and realistic as possible. Try to reproduce the subject as a real, living man or woman. Note the place and surroundings of the different events, e. g., Paul in Athens, Corinth, Philippi. Note the time relations of the different events. Very few people, in reading the Acts of the Apostles, for example, take notice of the rapid passage of time, and so regard events separated by years as following one another in close sequence. In this connection, note the age or approximate age of the subject at the time of the events recorded of him.

13. Summarize the lessons we should learn from the story of this person's life.

14. Note the person's relation to Jesus.

For example: as a type of Christ (Joseph, David, Solomon and others), forerunner of Christ, believer in Christ, enemy of Christ, servant of Christ, brother of Christ (James and Jude), friend, etc., etc.

It will be well to begin with some person who does not occupy too much space in the Bible, as, e.g., Enoch or Stephen. Of course many of the points mentioned above cannot be taken up with some characters.

Suggestive books in character studies are Stalker's *Lives of Christ and Paul,* and Stalker's *Imagio Christi;* Rev. F. B. Meyer's *Elijah,* and also other Old Testament characters; Mr. Moody's *Bible Characters.*

CHAPTER 5

Study of Types

A fourth method of study is the study of *types*. We have illustrations of this in the Bible itself, as for example in the epistle to the Hebrews. It is both an interesting and instructive method of study. It shows us the most precious truths buried away in what once seemed to us a very dry and meaningless portion of the Bible. It need scarcely be said that this method of study is greatly abused and overdone in some quarters. But that is no reason why we should neglect it altogether, especially when we remember that not only Paul but Jesus were fond of this method of study. The following may serve as principles to govern us in this method of study:

1. Be sure you have Bible warrant for your supposed type.

If one gives free rein to his fancy in this matter, he can imagine types everywhere, even in places that neither the human or divine author of the book had any intention of a typical sense. Never say this is a type unless you can point to some clear passage of Scripture where the truth said to be typified is definitely taught.

2. Begin with the more simple and evident types.

For example: the Passover (compare Ex. 12 with 1 Cor. 5:7, etc.), the High Priest, the Tabernacle.

3. Be on your guard against the fanciful and over-strained.

Fancy is almost sure to run away with any man who is blessed with any imagination and quickness of typical discernment, unless he holds it in check. Our typical sensitiveness will become both quickened and chastened by careful and circumspect exercise.

4. In studying any passage of possible typical suggestion, look up all the Scripture references.

The best collection of references is that given in *The Treasury of Scripture Knowledge.*

5. Study carefully the meaning of the names of persons and places mentioned.

Bible names often have a very deep and far reaching suggestiveness. Thus, for example, Hebron, which means "joining together," "union" or "fellowship," is deeply significant when taken in connection with its history, as are all the names of the Cities of Refuge, and indeed very many Scripture names. Was it accidental that Bethlehem, the name of the place where the Bread of Life was born, means "House of bread"?

C. H. M.'s notes on Genesis, Exodus, Leviticus, Numbers and Deuteronomy are suggestive to one who has had little experience in the study of types.

CHAPTER 6

The Study of the Books of the Bible in the Order Given in the Bible and in Their Chronological Order

A fifth method of the Bible study is the old fashioned method of the *study of the Bible in course*, beginning at Genesis and going right on until Revelation is finished. This method of study is ridiculed a good deal in these days, but it has some advantages which no other method of study possesses. It is sometimes said, you might as well begin at the top shelf of your library and read right through, as to begin at the beginning of the library of sixty-six books and read right through. To this it is a sufficient answer, "If you had a library that it was important to master as a whole, that you might understand the separate books in it, and that was as well arranged as the Bible is, then this method of going through your library would be excellent."

There are many advantages of studying in the Bible in course.

First, *it is the only method by which you will get an idea of the Book as a whole*. The more we know of the Bible as a whole, the better prepared we are for the understanding of any individual portion of it.

It is the only method by which you are likely to cover the whole book, and so take in the entire scope of God's revelation. It will be many a long year before any man covers the whole Bible by book studies, or even by topical studies. Every part of God's word is precious, and there are gems of truth hidden away in most unexpected places, e.g., 1 Chron. 4:10, where we hit upon these priceless gems by studying the Bible in course.

It is the best method to enable one to get hold of the unity of the Bible and its organic character.

It is a great corrective to one-sidedness and crankiness. The Bible is a many-sided book, it is Calvinistic and Arminian; it is Trinitarian and Unitarian, it clearly teaches the deity of Christ and insists on His real humanity, it exalts faith and demands works, it urges to victory through conflict and asserts most vigorously that victory is won by faith, etc., etc. If we become too much taken up with any one line of truth in our book or topical studies (and we are more than likely to), the daily study of the Bible in course will soon bring us to some contrasted line of truth, and bring us back to our proper balance. Some people go insane through becoming too much occupied with a single line of truth. The thoughtful study of the whole Bible is a great corrective to this tendency.

It would be well to have three methods of study in progress at the same time: first, the study of some book; second, the study of topics (perhaps topics suggested by the book studies); third, the study of the Bible in course. Every other method of study should be supplemented by studying the Bible in course.

Some yeas ago I determined to read the AV through every year, the RV through every year, and the New Testament in Greek through every year. It has proved exceedingly profitable, and I would not willingly give it up.

A sixth method of study is closely related to the fifth method and has advantages of its own that will appear as soon as the method is described. It is *studying the various portions of the Bible in their chronological order.* In this way the Psalms are read in their historical settings, as are prophecies, epistles, etc. The whole Bible has been excellently arranged for *chronological*

study in Miss Petrie's *Clews to Holy Writ.* (American Tract Society.) The course as outlined by Miss Petrie covers three years, and there are questions given for study and examination.

CHAPTER 7

The Study of the Bible for Practical Usefulness in Dealing with Men

The seventh and last method of study is *the study of the Bible for practical usefulness in dealing with men.*

To study the Bible in this way, make as complete a classification as possible of all the classes of men that one will meet. Write the names of the various classes at the head of separate sheets of paper or cards. Then begin the Bible and read it through slowly, and when you come to a passage that seems likely to prove useful in dealing with any class write it down upon its appropriate sheet. Go through the Bible in this way. It would be well to have a special Bible for this purpose, and have different colored inks, or different classes and underscore the texts with the proper colored ink, or mark it with the appropriate symbol. The results of the labors of others in this line can be found in a number of books, such as Munhall's *Furnishing for Workers*, Alexander Paterson's *Bible Manual for Christian Workers*, Drury's *HandBook for Workers*, and the author's *Vest Pocket Companion for Christian Workers* and his book, *How to Bring Men to Christ*. But the best book is the one you get up yourself. The books mentioned will give you suggestions how to do it. As a suggestion for beginning in the work, we give a list of classes of men, to which you can add for yourself.

Some Types of People

The careless and indifferent.

Those who wish to be saved but do not know how.

Those who know how to be saved but have difficulties.

"I am too great a sinner"

"My heart is too hard"

"I must become better before I become a Christian."

"I am afraid I can't hold out."

"I am too weak."

"I have tried before and failed."

"I can not give up my evil ways."

"I will be persecuted if I become a Christian."

"It will hurt my business."

"There is too much to give up."

"The Christian life is too hard."

"I am afraid of ridicule."

"I will lose my friends."

"I have no feeling."

"I have been seeking Christ, but cannot find Him."

"I have sinned away the day of grace."

"God won't receive me."

"I have committed the unpardonable sin."

"It is too late."

"Christians are so inconsistent."

"God seems to me unjust and cruel."

"There are so many things in the Bible which I can't understand."

"There is someone I can't forgive."

Those who are cherishing false hopes.

The hope of being saved by a righteous life.

The hope that "God is too good to damn anyone."

The hope of being saved by "trying to be a Christian."

The hope of being saved, because "I feel saved," or "I feel I am going to heaven."

The hope of being saved by a profession of religion, or church membership, or a faith, that does not save from sin.

Those who lack assurance.

Backsliders.

Skeptics.

Infidels.

Those who wish to put off the decision.

Roman Catholics.

Jews.

Spiritualists.

Christian Scientists.

Secret disciples.

The sorrowing.

The persecuted.

The despondent

The discouraged.

The morbid.

Worldly Christians.

The stingy.

The results of this work will be of incalculable value. In the first place, you will get a new view of how perfectly the Bible is adapted to every man's need. In the second place, familiar passages of the Bible will get a new meaning as you see their relation to the needs of men. The Bible will become a very living book. In the third place, in seeking food for others you will be fed yourself. And in the fourth place, you will get a vast amount of material to use in sermons, Bible readings, prayer meeting talks, and personal work. You will acquire a rare working knowledge of the Bible.

Part II

Fundamental Conditions of Profitable Bible Study

CHAPTER 1

Fundamental Conditions of the Most Profitable Bible Study

W e have considered seven profitable methods of Bible study. There is something, however, in Bible study more important than the best methods, that is, *the fundamental conditions of profitable study*. The one who meets these conditions will get more out of the Bible, while pursuing the poorest method, than the one who does not meet them will, while pursuing the best method. Many a one who is eagerly asking, "What method shall I pursue in my Bible study?" needs something that goes far deeper than a new and better method.

1. Be Born Again

The first of the fundamental conditions of the most profitable Bible study is *the student must be born again*. The Bible is a spiritual book: it "combines spiritual things with spiritual words" (I Cor. 2:13 RV Am. Ap.), and only a spiritual man can understand its deepest and most characteristic and most precious teachings. "The natural man receiveth not the things of the Spirit of God: for they are foolishness unto him; and he cannot know them, because they are spiritually judged." (1 Cor. 2:14RV)

Spiritual discernment can be obtained in but one way, by being born again. "Except a man be born anew, he cannot *see* the kingdom of God." (John 3:3 RV) No mere knowledge of the human languages in which the Bible was written, however extensive and accurate it may be, will qualify one to understand and appreciate the Bible. One must understand the divine language in which it was written as well—the language of the Holy Spirit. A person who understands the language of the Holy Spirit, but who does not understand a word of Greek or Hebrew of Aramaic, will get more out of the Bible, than one, who knows all about Greek, and Hebrew and cognate languages, but is not born again, and consequently, does not understand the language of the Holy Spirit.

It is a well demonstrated fact that many plain men and women who are entirely innocent of any knowledge of the original tongues in which the Bible was written, have a knowledge of the real contents of the Bible, its actual teaching, in its depth and fullness and beauty, that surpasses that of many learned professors in theological faculties.

One of the greatest follies of the day is to set unregenerate men to teaching the Bible, because of their rare knowledge of the human forms of speech in which the book was written. It would be as reasonable to set a man to teach art because he had an accurate technical knowledge of paints. It requires aesthetic sense to make a man a competent teacher of art. It requires spiritual sense to make a man a competent teacher of the Bible.

The man who had aesthetic discernment, but little or no technical knowledge of paint, would be a far more competent critic of works of art, than a man, who had a great technical knowledge of paint, but no aesthetic discernment; and so the man who has not technical knowledge of Greek and Hebrew, but who has spiritual discernment, is a far more competent critic of the Bible than the one who has a rare technical knowledge of Greek and Hebrew, but no spiritual discernment. It is exceedingly unfortunate that, in some quarters, more emphasis is laid upon a knowledge of Greek and Hebrew, in training for the ministry, than is laid upon spiritual life and its consequent spiritual discernment.

Unregenerate men should not be forbidden to study the Bible; for the Word of God is the instrument the Holy Spirit uses in the New Birth (1 Pet. 1:23; James 1:18): but it should be distinctly understood, that, while there are teachings in the Bible that the natural man can understand, and beauties which he can see, its most distinctive and characteristic teachings are beyond his grasp, and its highest beauties belong to a world in which he has no vision. The first fundamental condition of the most profitable Bible study, is, then, "Ye must be born again." You cannot study the Bible to the greatest profit if you have not been born again. Its best treasures are sealed to you.

2. Love the Bible

The second condition of the most profitable study is *a love for the Bible*. A man who eats with an appetite will get far more good out of his meal than a man who eats from a sense of duty. It is well when a student of the Bible can say with Job, "I have treasured up the words of his mouth more than my necessary food, " (Job 23:12 RV) or with Jeremiah, "Thy words were found and I did eat them; and thy words were unto me a joy and the rejoicing of mine heart; for I am called by thy name, O, Lord God of hosts." (Jer. 15:16 RV)

Many come to the table God has spread in His word with no appetite for spiritual food, and go mincing here and there and grumbling about everything. Spiritual indigestion lies at the bottom of much modern criticism of the Bible. But how can one get a love for the Bible? First of all, by being born again. Where there is life there is likely to be appetite. A dead man never hungers. This brings us back to the first condition. By going beyond this, the more there is of vitality the more there is of hunger. Abounding life means abounding hunger for the Word.

Study of the Word stimulates love for the Word. The author can well remember the time when he had more appetite for books about the Bible than he had for the Bible itself, but with increasing study there has come increasing love for the Book. Bearing in mind who the author of the Book is, what its purpose is, what its power is, what the riches of its contents are, will go far toward stimulating a love and appetite for the Book.

3. Be Willing to Work

The third condition is *a willingness to do hard work.* Solomon has given a graphic picture of the Bible student who gets the most profit out of his study.

> My son, if thou wilt receive my words, and lay up my commandments with thee; so that thou incline thine ear unto wisdom, and apply thine heart to understanding; yea, if thou cry after discernment, and lift up thy voice for understanding; if thou *seek her as silver, and search for her as for hid treasures; then* shalt thou understand the fear of the Lord and find the knowledge of God. (Prov. 2:1–5 RV)

Now, seeking for silver and searching for hid treasures, means hard work, and the one who wishes to get not only the silver but the gold as well out of the Bible, and find its "hid treasures," must make up his mind to dig. It is not glancing at the Word, or reading the Word, but studying the Word, meditating upon the Word, pondering the Word, that brings the richest yields.

The reason why many get so little out of their Bible reading is simply because they are not willing to think. Intellectual laziness lies at the bottom of a large percent of fruitless Bible reading. People are constantly crying for new methods of Bible study, but what many of them wish is simply some method of Bible study by which they can get all the good out of the Bible without work. If someone could tell lazy Christians some method of Bible study whereby they could put the sleepiest ten minutes of the day, just before they go to bed, into Bible study, and get the profit out of it that God intends His children shall get out of the study of His Word, that would be just what they desire. But it can't be done.

Men must be willing to work and work hard, if they wish to dig out the treasures of infinite wisdom and knowledge and blessing which He has stored up in His Word. A business friend once asked me in a hurried call to tell him "in a word" how to study his Bible. I replied, "Think."

The Psalmist pronounces that man "blessed" who "*meditates* in the law of the Lord, *day and night.*" (Ps. 1:2) The Lord commanded Joshua to "*meditate therein day and night,*" and assured him that as a result of this meditation "*then* thou shalt make thy way prosperous, and *then* thou shalt have good success." (Josh. 1:8) Of Mary, the mother of Jesus, we read, "Mary kept all these sayings, pondering them in her heart." (Luke 2:19 RV) In this way alone can one study the Bible to the greatest profit. One pound of beef well chewed and digested and assimilated, will give more strength than tons of beef merely glanced at; and one verse of scripture chewed and digested and assimilated, will give more strength than whole chapters simply skimmed.

Weigh every word you read in the Bible. Look at it. Turn it over and over. The most familiar passages get a new meaning in this way. Spend fifteen minutes on each word in Ps. 23:1, or Phil. 4:19, and see if it is not so.

4. Surrender Your Will Wholly to God

The fourth condition is *a will wholly surrendered to God.* Jesus said, "If any man willeth to do his will he shall know of the teaching." (Jn. 7:17 RV) A surrendered will gives that clearness of spiritual vision which is necessary to understand God's book. Many of the difficulties and obscurities of the Bible rise wholly from the fact that the will of the student is not surrendered to the will of the author of the Book.

It is remarkable how clear and simple and beautiful passages that once puzzled us become, when we are brought to that place where we say to God, "I surrender my will unconditionally to Thine. I have no will but Thine. Teach me Thy will." A surrendered will, will do more to make the Bible an open book than a university education. It is simply impossible to get the largest profit out of your Bible study until you do surrender your will to God. You must be very definite about this. There are many who say, "Oh, yes, my will, I think, is surrendered to God," and yet it is not. They have never gone alone with God and said intelligently and definitely to him, "O God, I here and now give myself up to Thee, for Thee to command me, and lead me, and shape me, and send me, and do with me, absolutely as Thou wilt." Such an act is a wonderful key to unlock the treasure house of God's Word. The Bible becomes a new book when a man does that. Doing that wrought a complete transformation in the author's theology and life and ministry.

5. Obey the Bible's Teachings

The fifth condition is very closely related to the fourth. *The student of the Bible who would get the greatest profit out of his studies must be obedient to its teachings as soon as he sees them.* It was good advice James gave to early

159

Christians, and to us: "Be ye *doers of the word,* and not hearers only, deceiving your own selves." (Jas. 1:22) There are a good many who consider themselves Bible students, who are deceiving themselves in this way today. They see what the Bible teaches, but they do not do it, and they soon lose their power to see it.

Truth obeyed leads to more truth. Truth disobeyed destroys the capacity for discovering truth. There must be not only a general surrender of the will, but specific practical obedience to each new word of God discovered. There is no place where the law—"unto every one that hath shall be given, and he shall have abundance; but from him that hath not shall be taken away even that which he hath,"—is more joyously certain on the one hand and more sternly inexorable on the other, than in the matter of using or refusing the truth revealed in the Bible. Use, and you get more; refuse, and you lose all.

Do not study the Bible for the mere gratification of intellectual curiosity, but to find out how to live and to please God. Whatever duty you find commanded in the Bible, do it at once. Whatever good you see in any Bible character, imitate it immediately. Whatever mistake you note in the actions of Bible men and women, scrutinize your own life to see if you are making the same mistake, and if you find you are, correct it forthwith. James compares the Bible to a looking glass. (Jas. 1:23, 24). The chief good of a looking glass is to show you if there is anything out of fix about you, and so, if you find that there is, you can set it right. Use the Bible in that way.

Obeying the truth you already see will solve the enigmas in the verses you do not as yet understand. Disobeying the truth you see darkens the whole world of truth. This is the secret of much of the skepticism and error of the day. Men saw the truth, but did not do it: now it is gone.

I knew a bright and promising young minister. He made rapid advancement in the truth. He took very advanced ground upon one point especially, and the storm came. One day he said to his wife, "It is very nice to believe this, but we need not speak so much about it." They began, or he, at least, to hide their testimony. The wife died and he drifted. The Bible became to him a sealed book. Faith reeled. He publicly renounced his faith in some of the fundamental truths of the Bible. He seemed to lose his grip even on the doctrine of immortality. What was the cause of it all? Truth not lived and stood for, flees. That man is much admired and applauded by some today, but daylight has given place to darkness in his soul.

6. Have a Child-Like Mind

The sixth condition is *a child-like mind.* God reveals His deepest truths to babes. No age needs more than our own to lay to heart the words of Jesus, "I thank thee, O Father, Lord of Heaven and earth, because Thou has hid these things from the wise and prudent, and has revealed them unto babes." (Matt 11:25)

Wherein must we be babes if God is to reveal His truth unto us, and we are to understand His Word? A child is not full of its own wisdom. It recognizes its ignorance and is ready to be taught. It does not oppose its own notions and ideas to those of its teachers. It is in that spirit we should come to the Bible, if we are to get the most profit out of our study.

Do not come to the Bible full of your own ideas, and seeking from it a confirmation of them. Come rather to find out what are God's ideas as He has revealed them there. Come not to find a confirmation of your own opinion, but to be taught what God may be pleased to teach. If a man comes to the Bible just to find his notions taught there, he will find them; but if he comes, recognizing his own ignorance, just as a little child, to be taught, he will find something infinitely better than his own notions—even the mind of God.

We see why it is that many persons cannot see things which are plainly taught in the Bible. The doctrine taught is not their notion, of which they are so full that there is no room left for that which the Bible actually teaches.

We have an illustration of this in the apostles themselves at one stage in their training. In Mark 9:31 we read "he taught his disciples, and said unto them, 'The Son of Man is delivered into the hands of men, and they shall kill Him; and after that he is killed, he shall rise the third day.'" Now, that is as plain and definite as language can make it, but it was utterly contrary to the notions of the apostles as to what was to happen to the Christ. So we read in the next verse "they understood not that saying." Is not that wonderful? But is it any more wonderful than our own inability to comprehend plain statements in the Bible when they run counter to our preconceived notions?

What trouble many Christians find with portions of the Sermon on the Mount that would be plain enough, if we just came to Christ like a child to be taught what to believe and do, rather than coming as full grown men who already know it all, and who must find some interpretations of Christ's words that will fit into our mature and infallible philosophy. Many a man is so full of an unbiblical theology he has been taught that it takes him a lifetime to get rid of it, and understand the clear teaching of the Bible. "Oh, what can this verse mean?" many a bewildered man cries. Why, it means what it plainly says; but what you are after is not the meaning God has manifestly put into it, but the meaning you can by some ingenious trick of exegesis twist out of it, and make it fit into your scheme.

Don't come to the Bible to find out what you can make it mean, but to find out what God intended it to mean. Men often miss the real truth of a verse by saying, "But that can be interpreted this way." Oh, yes, so it can, but is that the way God intended it to be interpreted? We all need to pray often, if we would get the most profit out of our Bible study:

> Oh, God, make me a little child. Empty me of my own notions. Teach me thine own mind. Make me ready like a little child to receive all that thou hast to say, no matter how contrary it is to what I have thought hitherto.

How the Bible opens up to one who approaches it in that way! How it closes up to the wise fool who thinks he knows everything, and imagines he can give points to Peter and Paul, and even Jesus Christ and to God Himself!

Someone has well said the best method of Bible study is "the baby method." I was once talking with a ministerial friend about what seemed to be the clear teaching of a certain passage. "Yes," he replied, "but that doesn't agree with my philosophy." Alas! But this man was sincere, yet he did not have the child-like spirit, which is an essential condition of the most profitable Bible study. But there are many who approach the Bible in the same way.

It is a great point gained in Bible study when we are brought to realize that an infinite God knows more than we, that indeed our highest wisdom is less than the knowledge of the most ignorant babe compared with His, and when we come to Him as babes, just to be taught by Him, and not to

162

argue with Him. But we so easily and so constantly forget this, that every time we open our Bibles we would do well to get down humbly before God and say, "Father, I am but a child, teach me."

This leads to the seventh condition.

7. Study the Bible as the Word of God

The seventh condition of studying the Bible to the greatest profit is that we *study it as the word of God.* The Apostle Paul, in writing to the Church of the Thessalonians, thanked God without ceasing that when they received the word of God they "accepted it not as the word of men, but as it is in truth the word of God." (1 Thess. 2:13 RV) Well might he thank God for that, and well may we thank God when we get to the place where we receive the word of God *as the word of God.*

Not that the one who does not believe the Bible is the word of God should be discouraged from studying it. Indeed, one of the best things that one who does not believe that the Bible is the word of God can do, if he is honest, is to study it. The author of this book once doubted utterly that the Bible was the word of God, and the firm confidence that he has today that the Bible is the Word of God has come more from the study of the book itself than from anything else. Those who doubt it are more usually those who study *about* the book, than those who dig into the actual teachings of the Book itself.

But while the best book of Christian evidences is the Bible, and while the most utter skeptic should be encouraged to study it, we will not get the largest measure of profit out of that study until we reach the point where we become convinced that the Bible is God's Word, and when we study it as such. There is a great difference between *believing theoretically* that the Bible is God's Word and *studying it as* God's Word. Thousands would tell you that they believe the Bible is God's Word, who do not study it as God's Word. Studying the Bible as the Word of God involves four things.

A. *Unquestioningly Accept the Bible's Clear Teachings*

First, it involves the unquestioning acceptance of its teachings when definitely ascertained, even when they may appear unreasonable or impossible. Reason demands that we submit our judgment and reasoning to the statements of infinite wisdom. There is nothing more irrational than rationalism, which makes the finite wisdom the test of infinite wisdom, and submits the teachings of God's omniscience to the approval of man's judgment. It is the sublimest and absurdest conceit that says, "This cannot be true, though God says it, for it does not approve itself to *my* reason." "Nay, but O man who art thou, that repliest against God?" (Rom. 9:20)

Real human wisdom, when it finds infinite wisdom, bows before it and says, "Speak what thou wilt and I will believe." When we have once become convinced that the Bible is God's Word, its teachings must be the end of all controversy and discussion. A "thus saith the Lord" will settle every question. Yet there are many who profess to believe that the Bible is the Word of God, and if you show them what the Bible clearly teaches on some disputed point, they will shake their heads and say, "Yes, but I *think* so and so," or "Doctor —, or Prof. This, or our church, don't teach that way." There is little profit in that sort of Bible study.

B. Absolutely Rely on the Bible's Promises

Studying the Bible as the word of God involves, in the second place, absolute reliance upon all its promises in all their length and breadth. The man who studies the Bible as the word of God will not discount any one of its promises one iota.

The one who studies the Bible as the Word of God will say, "God, who cannot lie, has promised," and will not try to make God a liar by trying to make one of his promises mean less than it says. The one who studies the Bible as the word of God, will be on the lookout for promises, and as soon as he finds one, he will seek to ascertain just what it means, and, as soon as he discovers, he will step right out upon that promise, and risk everything upon its full import. That is one of the secrets of profitable Bible study. Be hunting for promises and appropriate them as fast as you find them—this is done by meeting the conditions and risking all upon them. That is the way to make your own all the fullness of blessing God has for you. This is the key to all the treasures of God's grace. Happy is the man who has so learned to study the Bible as God's word, that he is ready to claim for himself every new promise as it appears, and to risk everything upon it.

C. Prompt Obedience to the Bible's Commands

Studying the Bible as the Word of God involves, in the third place, obedience—prompt, exact obedience, without asking any questions—to its every precept. Obedience may seem hard, it may seem impossible: but God has bidden it and I have nothing to do but obey, and leave the results with God. If you would get the very most profit out of your Bible study, resolve that from this time you will claim every clear promise and obey every plain command, and that as to the promises and commands whose import is not yet clear, you will try to get their meaning made clear.

D. Study the Bible As If in God's Presence

Studying the Bible as the Word of God involves, in the fourth place, studying it as in God's presence. When you read a verse of scripture, hear the voice of the living God speaking directly to you in these written words. There is new power and attractiveness in the Bible when you have learned to hear a living, present person—God, our Father, Himself—talking directly to you in these words.

One of the most fascinating and inspiring statements in the Bible is, "Enoch walked with God." (Gen. 5:24.) We can have God's glorious companionship any moment we please, by simply opening His Word and letting the living and ever present God speak to us through it. With what holy awe and strange and unutterable joy one studies the Bible if he studies it in this way! It is heaven come down to earth.

8. Be Prayerful

The eighth and last condition of the most profitable Bible study is *prayerfulness*. The Psalmist prayed, "Open thou mine eyes, that I may behold wondrous things out of thy law." (Ps. 119:18) Every one who desires to get the greatest profit out of his Bible study needs to offer that or a similar prayer every time he undertakes the study of the word. Few keys open so many caskets that contain hidden treasure as prayer. Few clues unravel so many difficulties. Few microscopes will disclose so many beauties hidden from the eye of the ordinary observer.

What new light often shines from an old familiar text as you bend over it in prayer! I believe in studying the Bible a good deal on your knees. When one reads an entire book through upon his knees—and this is easily done—that book has a new meaning, and becomes a new book. One ought never to open the Bible to read it without at least lifting the heart to God in silent prayer that He will interpret it, illumine its pages by the light of His Spirit.

It is a rare privilege to study any book under the immediate guidance and instruction of its author, and this is the privilege of us all in studying the Bible.

When one comes to a passage that is difficult to understand or difficult to interpret, instead of giving it up, or rushing to some learned friend, or to some commentary, he should lay that passage before God, and ask Him to explain it to him, pleading God's promise, "if any of you lack wisdom, let him ask of *God*, that giveth to all men liberally, and upbraideth not, and it shall be given him. But let him ask in faith, nothing doubting." (Jas. 1:5, 6 RV)

It is simply wonderful how the seemingly most difficult passages become plain by this treatment. Harry Morehouse, one of the most remarkable Bible scholars among unlearned men, used to say that whenever he came to a passage in the Bible which he could not understand, he would search through the Bible for some other passage that threw light upon it, and lay it before God in prayer—and that he had never found a passage that did not yield to this treatment.

The author of this book has had a quite similar experience. Some years ago I was making with a friend a tour by foot of the Franconian Switzerland, and visiting some of the more famous zoolithic caves. One day the country letter-carrier stopped us, and asked if we would not like to see a cave of rare beauty and interest, away from the beaten tracks of travel. Of course, we said yes.

He led us through the woods and underbrush to the mouth of the cave, and we entered. All was dark and uncanny. He expatiated greatly [talked at length] on the beauty of the cave, telling us of altars and fantastic formations, but we could see absolutely nothing. Now and then he uttered a note to warn us to have a care, as near our feet lay a gulf, the bottom of which had never been discovered. We began to have a fear that we might be the first discoverers of the bottom. There was nothing pleasant about the whole affair.

But as soon as a magnesian taper was lighted, all became different. There were the stalagmites rising from the floor to meet the stalactites as they came down from the ceiling. There was the great altar of nature, that peasant fancy ascribed to the skill of ancient worshipers; there were the beautiful and fantastic formations on every hand, and all glistening in fairy-like beauty in the brilliant light.

So I have often thought it was with many a passage of Scripture. Others tell you of its beauty, but you cannot see it. It looks dark and intricate and forbidding and dangerous, but when God's own light is kindled there by prayer, how different all becomes in an instant. You see a beauty that language cannot express, and that those alone can appreciate, who have stood there in the same light.

He who would understand and love his Bible must be much in prayer. Prayer will do more than a college education to make the Bible an open and glorious book. Perhaps the best lesson I learned in a German university, where I had the privilege of receiving the instruction of one of the most noted and most gifted Bible teachers of any age, was that which came though the statement of the famulus [secretary] of this professor, that Professor Delitzsch worked out much of his teaching upon his knees.

CHAPTER 2

Final Suggestions

There are some suggestions that remain to be given before we close this book.

1. Study the Bible daily.

Regularity counts for more in Bible study than most people fancy. The spasmodic student, who at certain seasons gives a great deal of time to the study of the Word, and at other seasons quite neglects it, even for days at a time, does not achieve the results that he does, who plods on regularly day by day. The Bereans were wise as well as "noble" in that they "searched the scriptures daily." (Acts 17:2; see also RV.)

A man who is well known among the Christian college students of America once remarked at a student convention, that he had been at many conventions and had received great blessings from them, but the greatest blessing he had ever received was from a convention where there were only four persons gathered together. The blessing had come to him in this way. These four had covenanted together to spend a certain portion of every day in Bible study. Since that day, much of his time had been spent on the cars or in hotels and at conventions, but he had tried to keep that covenant, and the greatest blessing that had come to him in his Christian life, had come through this *daily* study of the Word.

No one who has not tried it realizes how much can be accomplished by setting apart a fixed portion of each day—it may not be more than fifteen or thirty minutes, but it surely *should* be an hour—for Bible study, and keeping it sacredly for that purpose, under all circumstances.

Many will say, "I cannot spare the time. It will be time saved. Lord Cairnes, one of the busiest as well as most eminent men of his day, before his death testified that the first two hours of every day were given to the study of the Bible and prayer, and he attributed the great achievements of his life to that fact.

It will not do to study the Bible only when we feel like it. It will not do to study the Bible only when we have leisure. We must have fixed principles and habits in this matter, if we are to study the Bible to the greatest profit. Nothing that we do will be more important than our Bible study, and it cannot give way to other less important things. What regularity in eating is to physical life, regularity in Bible study is to spiritual life. Fix upon some time, even if it is no more than fifteen minutes to start with, and hold to it until you are ready to set a longer period.

2. Select for your Bible study the best portion of the day that you can give to it.

Do not put your Bible study off until nearly bedtime, when the mind is drowsy. It is well to take a parting verse for the day, when one retires for the night, but this is not the time for study. No study demands all that there is in a man, as Bible study does. Do not take the time immediately after a heavy meal. The mind is more or less torpid after a heavy meal, and it is unwise to put it on the stretch then.

It is almost the unanimous opinion of those who have given this subject careful attention, that the early hours of the day are the best for Bible study, if they can be secured free from interruption. It is well, wherever possible, to lock yourself in and lock the world out, when you are about to give yourself up to the study of the Bible.

3. In all your Bible study, look for Christ in the passage under examination.

We read of Jesus that, "beginning at Moses and all the prophets, he expounded unto them *in all the Scriptures* the things concerning *Himself*." (Luke 24:27) Jesus Christ is the subject of the whole Bible, and the subject pervades the book. Some of the seemingly driest portions of the Bible become instinct [imbued] with a new life when we learn to see Christ in them.

I remember in my early reading of the Bible what a stupid book Leviticus seemed, but it all became different when I learned to see Jesus in the various offerings and sacrifices, in the high-priest and his garments, in the tabernacle and its furniture, indeed everywhere. Look for Christ in every verse you study, and even the genealogies and catalogues of the names of towns will begin to have beauty and power.

4. Memorize Scripture.

The Psalmist said, "Thy word have I laid up in mine heart, that I might not sin against thee." (Ps. 119:2 RV) There is nothing better to keep one from sinning than this. By the word of God laid up in His heart, Jesus overcame tempter. (Matt. 4:4, 7, 10)

But the word of God laid up in the heart is good for other purposes than victory over sin. It is good to meet and expose error; it is good to enable one "to speak a word in season to him that is weary." (Is. 1:4) It is good for manifold uses, even "that the man of God may be complete, furnished completely unto every good work." (2 Tim. 3:17 RV)

Memorize Scripture by chapter and verse. It is quite as easy as merely memorizing the words, and it is immeasurably more useful for practical purposes. Memorize the Scripture in systematic form. Do not have a chaotic heap of texts in the mind, but pigeonhole under appropriate titles the scripture you store in memory. Then you can bring it out when you need it, without racking your brains.

There are many men who can stand up without a moment's warning, and talk coherently and cogently and scripturally, on any vital theme; because they have a vast fund of wisdom in the form of scripture texts stored away in their mind in systematic form.

171

5. Finally, Utilize Spare Moments in the Study of the Bible.

In most men's lives there is a vast amount of wasted time. Time spent in traveling on the street cars and railroads; time spent in waiting for persons with whom they have engagements; time spent in waiting for meals, etc., etc. Most of this can be utilized in Bible study, if one carries with him a pocket Bible, or pocket Testament. Or, one can utilize it in meditation upon texts stored away in memory. Many of the author's sermons and addresses are worked out in that way.

It is said that Henry Ward Beecher read one of the larger histories of England through, while waiting day after day for his meals to be brought on to the table. How many books of the Bible could be studied in the same time?

A friend once told me that the man who had, in some respects, the most extraordinary knowledge of the Bible of any man he knew, was a junk dealer in a Canadian city. This man had a Bible open on his shelves, and in intervals of business he was pondering the Book of God. The book became very black by handling in such surroundings, but I have little doubt his soul became correspondingly white.

There is no economy that pays as does economy of time, but there is no way of economizing time so thriftily as putting the moments that are going to waste into the study of or meditation upon the Word of God.

How To Pray

How To Study The Bible

Patricia Klein wrote the series preface and provided editorial oversight.
The cover and interior were designed by Tina Donahue.
The text was copyedited and typeset by Patricia Ames.
Production was coordinated by Rick Brown and Ann F. Droppers.

The text of this book is set in Goudy Old Style and Goudy Small Caps,
with Woodtype Ornaments.